Empath

The Practical Survival Guide For Empaths And The Highly Sensitive Person To Thrive In The Modern World

Copyright 2019, Empath, Alexandra Jessen- All rights reserved.

In no way is it legal to reproduce, duplicate, or transmit any part of this document in either electronic means or in printed format. Recording of this publication is strictly prohibited and any storage of this document is not allowed unless with written permission from the author. All rights reserved.

Table of Contents

Chapter 01: Introduction 4

Chapter 02: The Game Of Energy 47

Chapter 03: Relationships 68

Chapter 04: Work and Career 109

Chapter 05: Empaths and Self Care 128

Chapter 06: Spirituality And Transcending Limitations As An Empath 174

Resources 199

Chapter 01: Introduction

Three years into my psychology degree, I couldn't take it anymore. I had to make a drastic decision about my life and where it was headed before I completely lost it!

Monday morning the alarm goes off at 6.20 am and I immediately get sucked into this feeling of dread. It's like a truck ran over me a dozen times during the night. I only had four hours of sleep, which I suppose is some progress from the three hours of sleep over the past three months. I literally feel and look like one of those characters from the walking dead, except much worse.No matter what I tell myself, getting out of bed just feels like punishment. The muscles in my body ache, yet I haven't been to the gym in months. I have this sick feeling in my stomach that feels like the flu, but I know I'm not ill.
In fact, that feeling follows me around everywhere lately, and it seems to be getting

worse on Mondays. In my head, I am already wishing the day would be over so I could just crawl under my sheets and cry over my exhausting life.

Going through my day at the campus was becoming more and more unbearable. Sitting in a group with my friends talking over some negative nonsense and school politics, I felt utterly alone and so misunderstood. Yes, school had never been easy for me (especially the socializing part), but somehow my encouraging mother led me to believe it does get better with time. No, mom, it doesn't.

One time a substitute professor came in to give a lecture, and as soon as she was done I was so nauseous I had to rush to the bathroom to barf. It took weeks before people stopped making fun of me for that incident. "You need to toughen up softy, or you'll never make it in life." they mocked.

Now I realize time does nothing to help someone like me. The bouts of depression that have been showing up ever since I hit my teenage years were never going to go away. No matter how hard I tried to escape, I would always circle back to another "winter season." Each time felt worse than the last. My health was all over the place. Some months I'd feel great, some months it was hellish.

I kept gaining and losing weight even when my diet remained the same. And the thought of spending one more year in a class with my insensitive professors who hardly seemed to understand anything about the human behavior (even though they receive accolades on the topic) made me sick to my gut. Something had to change...

That was my state five years ago. Life was tough. No. It was miserable! I was trying to do good by my parents, friends, teachers, and society, but realized I was destroying myself in the process. I was born into a caring family that valued logic and traditional education and was spending all my life proving my worth by pursuing goals that society deemed right.

Fast forward five years later, and I am a new person. I feel resurrected. A rebirth took place, and it's all because I stopped playing in the shadows. I stopped hiding the aspects of me that others struggled to understand. I quit apologizing for being so keenly aware of how everyone around me genuinely feels even when they try to mask their emotions. I started owning my weirdness, and it has paid off significantly. First, I discovered that I wasn't the only one who had this ability to "feel" people, animals, objects, and places in ways that the average individual can't. More on this in a few minutes.

I also discovered those like me (scattered all over the world) are taking a stand on their unique gifts and learned that some scientists are even starting to study us so they can better understand what makes our kind tick. It isn't that we are more "special" than other human beings; we are merely - different.

And when you know you're different, it becomes necessary to start thinking and living differently. Wouldn't you agree?

If you are still reading this and nodding along, that tells me you, and I share certain similarities. Whether you already know about your unique gifts or are starting to question more about who you really are, trust that you've come across this book at the right time. Regardless of how much struggle and suffering you've experienced in the past or how alone you've felt, I can promise you one thing: You are not alone.

Everything you've gone through has been preparing you to become the person you were meant to be in this lifetime. And the work that lies ahead of you now requires you to step into your power and embrace the real you. The one you probably don't yet fully understand. And that's okay because by the time you're done reading this book, that new you will emerge clear as day and you will finally find the peace and freedom you deserve.

This was my quest a few years ago when my heart had had enough of doing what everyone was doing. It is my intention that this book can offer you the solace and guidance you need to start thriving as the real and powerful you. Now, I know I'm making some big claims here, and I intend to live up to them, as that is part of my mission today. But having said that, I think it's also essential we set the right expectations. I wouldn't want you to have misconceptions about what this book can do for you.

What This Book Is Not.

This isn't going to be one of those books on empaths that makes it okay for you to continue hiding in the shadows. I know most empaths have been led to believe that the best thing they can do is avoid people, protect themselves from outside forces and accept suffering as a way of life. Most teachings on empaths are about finding coping mechanisms. In other words, there's nothing you can do about your current life so just accept things as they as. This is not one of those books. There's plenty of material to support that mindset if that's more your cup of tea, so I recommend you find that type of message elsewhere.

But here's what I can assure you this book can and will do for you if you let it.
You can finally find practical tools, insights, and processes to help you step out of that lifestyle of quiet desperation and suffering. If you've had enough of that shared experience of

being fragile and at the mercy of everyone else's "stuff" then you're ready to consume the content in this book and transform your life. Your health, relationships, career and sense of self-worth can finally transform and become what you've always wanted them to be. Wanna know why?

Because the core message of this book is to take you from a coping surviving empath to a thriving one. That means no more settling for being a doormat or a dumping ground for other people. It means no more giving away your power. Most importantly, it means changing your perception about yourself and what it means to go through life as an empath. If that's what you've been seeking, then take a deep breath, relax and allow the transformation to begin.

What Is An Empath?

Although this is still a term being developed (especially when it comes to scientific studies), we can apply the following working definition: An empath is a person who detects, processes and can absorb the emotions and energies that surround them (if they choose to). This can be from other people, the environment and animals. It's a heightened level of sensitivity, empathy, and compassion. An empath can pick up another person's feelings, physical sensations and can even sense someone's spiritual orientation.

We are highly intuitive, sensitive and caring but we are also like shock absorbers with an extremely porous nervous system and hyperactive reflexes. Our experience of pleasure and pain is so intense and can sometimes become overwhelming.

Let me ask you this... Have you spent all your life being told that you're "too sensitive" or that you need to grow thicker skin?

That's all I heard growing up. I would walk into a mall perfectly fine and walk out with aches and pains that came from who knows where! A day at the mall was something I didn't enjoy because I knew it would take me a whole evening (sometimes an entire day) just to recover from the energy drain and strange aches I had picked up. I realized early in my life that being in large crowds or hanging out with certain people exhausted me. And then there was the strange sensation and overload I experienced with bright lights, loud noises, and heavy smells, but I'll share more about that discovery a little later in the book. For now, I want you to see that being an empath is more than just having compassion and caring about others. It is true we approach fellow human beings, animals and our environment different from other people, but it's far more than that.

There are certain subtle experiences going on within us, and the more we become aware of what they mean, the better control we can have over our lives.

Many empaths also possess certain natural gifts whether they are aware of it or not and in my experience, much of the restlessness and constriction we tend to feel is because our undeveloped gifts are suffocating within trying to find a way out.

Is Empathy and Empath the same thing?

There is a connection between the two, but they are not one and the same. Empathy is when you are able to put yourself in the shoes of another. It is the ability to understand and share the feelings and thoughts that another is experiencing from his or her point of view. In other words, when you're being empathic, your heart goes out to someone else. You experience deep compassion.

Contemporary researchers are continuing to study this topic and have identified two types of empathy, namely: Affective and Cognitive empathy.
According to the Greater Good Science-based Magazine, "Affective empathy refers to the sensations and feelings we get in response to other's emotion. This can include mirroring what that person is feeling or just feeling stressed when we detect another's fear or anxiety. Cognitive empathy, on the other hand, refers to our ability to identify and understand other people's emotions."

Research is proving that empathy has deep roots in our brains and bodies. It is part of our evolutionary history as human beings, and in fact, we can observe some elementary forms of empathy even in dogs and rats. This leads me to believe that empathy is part of the true nature of every human being. However, there are those that have a more profound experience when it comes to connecting with fellow human beings and nature. We'll talk a bit more about the scientific findings around this topic as the chapters unfold but for now, what I want you to get is that while empathy is a quality inherent in all of us which can be developed and enhanced by those who choose to do so, empaths are individuals who experience more than just empathy and compassion for others.

An empath is capable of absorbing and embodying the feelings of another. I want you to imagine it as a spectrum. On this empathic spectrum, we have on one corner the empath, and as you move toward the middle, you have those that are known as highly sensitive people (we'll talk about that distinction in just a bit). Dr. Elaine Aron has called this group Highly Sensitive People (HSP), but they are not to be confused with empaths. As you move closer to the middle of the empathic spectrum, you'll find people with strong empathy who are not HSPs or empaths. Then as you move further away from the mid-point, toward the opposite side of the spectrum, you'll find sociopaths, psychopaths, and narcissists who are considered to have empath-deficient disorders.

As you can see, on the one extreme we have a person who experiences a heightened version of empathic abilities. Such a person will have a very different encounter going through their daily life and interacting with people. Move further away from that side, and you'll find the average individual who feels some empathy, but it certainly doesn't control their life. To the opposite extreme, you'll find those that have lost any ability to experience compassion. Such a person is considered to be the extreme opposite of the empath (a narcissist), and of course, we'll also talk more about this on the chapter of relationships.

Given the novelty of this topic, science doesn't yet give concrete differentiator between empathy and empaths. But those like me that are empaths can tell you that although empathy is the underlying quality in all of us, those of us who are high on that spectrum also posses other unique attributes that cause us to experience life, relationships and this planet in a different way.

Emerging Scientific Discoveries

Some scientists have been skeptical about whether empaths do really exist. They argue that there is no real evidence to support the claims that we make about our experience of life and others. It is true in the past there has been very little direct evidence, but I see things changing with time thankfully.

Science has proven that we have mirror neurons (a specialized group of cells that are responsible for compassion) in the brain, which are said to enable us to read and understand each other's emotions. For empaths, however, our brain's mirror neuron system is said to be hyperactive. This enables us to absorb other people's energies into our own bodies. The energy may, of course, be positive or negative depending on what we are exposed to.

Other studies used to explain empaths include the concept of emotional contagion which is the idea that when people synchronize, their attitudes, behaviors, and speech they also synchronize their emotions both consciously and unconsciously (Hatfield, Cacioppo & Rapson, 1994). Of course, even such studies don't really do a good job explaining empaths. But in recent years more direct evidence is beginning to be discovered.

Neuroscientist and psychologist Abigail Marsh wrote something intriguing in the book The Fear Factor. She found evidence that there is a difference in the brains of people who are highly empathic to others and called such individuals "altruists." Marsh was motivated to carry out this research based on personal experience, so she wanted to learn what causes people to engage in selfless acts even when there was no direct benefit or when there was a high cost involved. She worked with people who had been involved in the most extreme selfless act that fit into this category. Things like donating kidneys to complete strangers, often anonymously. Sounds like typical empath behavior to me...

Once she recruited the right people, she measured their brain activity while showing them pictures of faces with varying emotional expressions. Then she contrasted this with a control group of people who hadn't performed the same selfless act. For example, she took the people who donated the kidney and showed them varying facial expressions of other people and then showed the same to another control group that did not donate a kidney. The "altruists" were especially sensitive to fearful facial expressions, and when they recognized fear, there was heightened activity in the amygdalae in their brains. Marsh also found that the amygdalae of the "altruists" were 8% larger than those belonging to members of the control group.

Now it is important that I note that Marsh never refers to the altruists as empaths in her book. But if you look at the research, the traits she outlines and the responses she got from this group I believe empaths would be a perfect label. First, she reports that there are different types of altruism, including kin-based, reciprocity-based, and care-based (Marsh, 2016). In her research, she seems to focus more on care-based altruism where no reward or genetic reward to the self is expected. This type of behavior is driven by the concern for the wellbeing of others and nothing more.

Another surprising finding in Marsh's work is how she contrasts psychopaths. Usually, we tend to hear that empaths and psychopaths are polar opposites and Marsh actually refers to the altruist in her study as "anti-psychopaths" because of what her findings showed. When she examined brains of psychopaths the results were the exact opposite of the response garnered from the altruists. The psychopaths were less able to recognize fear on the faces of others and less responsive even when they did. And when it came to the size of their amygdalae, it was 8% smaller than normal.

In other words, psychopaths and altruists both have abnormal brains when it comes to responding to fear and reading facial expressions. The only difference is they are abnormal in opposite directions. This to me appears to support the concept of the empathy spectrum that we usually use. We still have a long way to go when it comes to scientific finding, but this seems like a good start to me.

Our experience and intuitive knowing as empaths are starting to receive some scientific backing. It is scientifically accurate that a psychopath will neither feel nor react to the fear of others while those of us who are empaths can't help but feel and move to respond to the fears of others as if they were our own.

The difference between an Empath and a highly sensitive person

Most highly sensitive people would qualify as empaths, but it is not a fact as they are not mutually exclusive. Both empaths and highly sensitive people share similar qualities such as the need for alone time, and high sensory sensitivity which means they are both super sensitive to sound, smell and light. Both have a low threshold for stimulation and in fact, takes them longer to wind down after a busy day. Highly sensitive people are usually introverts, but you can find both introverts and extroverts with empaths. Both share a deep connection and love of nature and always prefer quiet environments.

One of the core differences, however, is that as empaths we can take the experience of energy and emotions much further. We can sense very subtle energy, and we can absorb these energies from other people and the environment. Due to our ability to absorb into our bodies the energy around us, we sometimes have a hard time telling it apart from our own. And if the other person is experiencing pain, discomfort, joy or hurt, we can experience that same energy as if it were our own. This isn't something that a highly sensitive person would go through.

Again, let's go back to that imaginary empathic spectrum I spoke about, an empath would be at the far end (the extreme corner) of the spectrum whereas the highly sensitive person would be further in, closer to the middle of the spectrum where people with strong empathy reside.

Studies have shown that about fifteen to twenty percent of the population in the United States of America alone is comprised of highly sensitive people. Although it is related to being an introvert, there's more to it than that. For example, if you realize that you get easily overwhelmed when you have a lot to do or that you don't perform well in noisy environments and can't stand violent media, then it's very possible you are a highly sensitive person.

Being a highly sensitive person or an empath doesn't mean there's something wrong with you. It's certainly nothing to be ashamed of. You simply process information and data more deeply, and it's essential you recognize this so you can make adjustments in your lifestyle and work environment. Whether you are both an empath and a highly sensitive person or feel like you're only a highly sensitive person, this book will empower you with tools and practices that will help you thrive in all areas of life that matter to you so keep reading.

Different Types of Empaths

With empaths, you best believe there are varying types mostly depending on the personality type as well as the gifts they possess. But let's pause for a moment before jumping into categorization and allow me to share with you the main difference that exists within the empath community.

I firmly believe the main difference that is worthy of serious discussion is whether one is an empowered or disempowered empath.

An empowered empath:

This is an empath who is self-aware, knows his or her sensitivities, special talents and has learned to handle them positively. Such a person has developed his or her mental, emotional, physical and spiritual aspects and lives from a place of power. Being an empath is a gift, and they go through life on purpose, shining their light, thriving and making a difference in this world through these gifts.

When it comes to detecting and processing emotions and energy in their surrounding, they are masters. They not only do it without compromising their own state, they even know how to influence the energy around them and can often perform healing sessions quite effortlessly. To illustrate this type of empath, imagine yourself being an empowered empath walking into a room where friends are sitting exchanging the latest gossip. One of your friends isn't feeling too well. You immediately pick up on the negative vibes and process the information coming in as unwanted, so you dissolve that energy pattern and radiate outward more soothing energy. Although you choose to leave that gathering because you realize it won't be beneficial for you, the energy that you leave them with makes them say " I always feel so much better when you are around. I wish you could stay longer."

When you're an empowered empath, you have the power to influence the energy around you and help others feel better without getting caught up in their negative vibes.

A disempowered empath:
As you might have guessed, this is an empath who is still in the struggle and suffering phase. While they may know of their empathic abilities and special sensitivities, they certainly haven't developed themselves. Such a person feels powerless, at the mercy of others and probably hasn't found a way to make good use of their powers. Being an empath feels more like a curse and dealing with daily human living is a constant struggle. When it comes to detecting and processing emotions around them, they feel very fragile and incapable of controlling anything. This is why you'll hear

many people say empaths are emotional sponges at the mercy of energy vampires.

To illustrate this type of empath, all you have to do is type in the term on Google, and you'll find all kinds of examples. And even if I were to contrast from the empowered empath illustration, walking into a room with that same group of friends sending off that negative vibe would be a common occurrence and you'd probably find your mood changing, body aching and energy drained soon after hanging out with them. This is the information so many books, teachers and blogs leave out.

They are so focused on the suffering and struggles of being empaths they forget to mention that one always has the power of choice. You can choose whether to live your life as a disempowered or an empowered empath. If you can gain clarity on these two main differences, the rest of the book will carry many useful lessons and eye-openers that will enable you to step into a life you love living as an empath.

Now, let's get back to discussing the different categories that have been created within the empath community. Just know that things often get really complicated when trying to identify all the varieties of empaths that exist and I bet there are many more we are yet to uncover. But there is a main "umbrella" that covers all the different types with their unique gifts. This can be categorized into two: Introverted empaths (the majority within the empath group) and extroverted empaths.

Introverted and extroverted empaths might share similarities and even possess some of the same gifts, but their personalities will vary. And depending on which you are, your needs and how you recharge will be different. For example, I am an introverted empath. I love being on my own, connecting with my own energy and nature. I love space and solitude.

My way of refueling and recharging requires me to be on my own. Large crowdy places, big parties with lots of people are not a preference. I would rather have one on one interactions or small intimate groups. I need to be close to the water as much as possible.

I have a friend who is also an empath, but she's an example of an extroverted empath. She loves parties and doing dinner dates. I call her a social bird, and it really does suit her because whether she's at work, in the supermarket, at Starbucks or lining up at the bank, she's the girl always smiling and looking to start a conversation. Her way of refueling doesn't actually need time alone (like me). She is a deep sleeper and requires around ten hours of deep sleep, which is where she believes her refueling happens. So as you can see we are both empaths but certainly different in the way we express it and in how we relate to the world around us. Bottom line is that this will vary from one empath to the next depending on how he or she processes sensations, information, and energy.

Aside from that core personality based difference within empaths we also possess certain gifts that each of us were born with. These are talents hidden deep within us, and it is our job to uncover, develop and share these talents with the world. Sometimes, due to traumatic childhood experiences, our abilities get muted out, and we struggle to reconnect with that aspect of ourselves. I believe many empaths struggle with anxiety, low self-esteem, and reclusion because there's a disconnect between who they are authentically and the false conditioning that has become their daily life. When you learn to hide from the world all your life, that inner restlessness will always haunt you, but it's hard to pinpoint where it's coming from. That was part of my struggle as well so if you're having a hard time feeling like you are valuable, please be easy on yourself. It's a phase we all have to go through boldly, and the best way to do it is by becoming aware of your talent, developing it, turning it into a useful skill and courageously sharing it with the world. I'm going to be sharing with you an example of a girl who did just that and turned her negative situation into a six-figure business. I do it not to impress you with the idea of financial gain but because I want to impress upon you the importance of owning the talents that come naturally to you. The light that you shine in this world deserves to be known, and it was meant to be used in service to others.

This is why I want us to dive deeper into the different qualities and talents an empath might have. It is important to mention here that having talent is one thing, turning it into a skill is another. Your ability to earn a good living doing something you love and helping people out with whatever gift you possess depends on you developing your talent into an active skill. Although we are all diverse as empaths, the one thing we all have in common is each one of us comes with certain unique gifts. Find your gift, nurture it, develop it and share it generously in the world. Here are a few talents many empaths find themselves in possession of.

Spiritual Empath

A spiritual empath has direct connections to other realms. Most people refer to these types of empaths as mediums. They usually possess the ability to connect with spiritual beings from other realms, deceased human beings, and other spirits. They also tend to possess psychic empathic abilities that include being able to feel physical and emotional symptoms from their communication with the spiritual realm. It's similar to how an emotional empath can connect and sense with those in the physical realm, this empath connects with others in the spiritual world.

Earth Empath

This type of an empath is connected to the earth in a more than ordinary way. He or she can intuit the earth's changes consciously and at a very cellular level. If you are this type of an empath, then your experience of nature is anything but mundane. You can feel the power of the thunderstorm, and the warmth of the sun rests on your shoulders. The beauty and health of the earth nourishes and refuels you. The moon, the ocean, and tides affect everyone but especially you. The beauty and magnificence of a waterfall exhilarate you whereas air pollutants make you feel ill, exhausted and depressed. You are also sensitive to weather changes and the amount of daylight. As an earth empath, you are prone to Seasonal Affective Disorders (SAD), which makes you fall into depression or "catch the blues" during winter when days are shorter.

Physical empath

If you are a physical empath, then you've probably noticed that you can feel someone else's pain or anxiety in your body and that you usually have so many unexplained symptoms. You're chronically tired, and every time you see a doctor, the response is always the same. "You're fine, just get more rest." But you know something isn't quite right no matter what the doctors say. Empaths who are so porous and can't help but pick up other people's symptoms are what we call physical empaths. And I can tell you, this one is really tricky because you need to be very mindful and in control of your whole self whenever you're dealing with other people. Otherwise, you might walk into a restaurant for dinner with a new boyfriend and leave with a cold or fever even before dessert!

My friend Jenny recently had this experience, and it was the worst. She had been excited to go on a first date with this new guy for about three months and even bought a particular

"black dress" for the occasion. On the afternoon of the date when I saw her, she was perfectly healthy. By the time she called me later that night she was struggling to cure a fever that somehow took over right in the middle of her date. Ouch! As you can imagine, the night didn't go as perfectly as she had planned. In retracing her steps, she quickly realized she had paid close attention to a woman sitting near her table who didn't "feel" well or happy to Jenny. The woman was trying really hard to get through the night, but Jenny sensed her discomfort and anxiousness. It also seemed as though she was experiencing a terrible migraine and kept ordering more ice.
Unfortunately for Jenny, she started experiencing the same in her body, and before she knew it, her palms were sweaty, she couldn't breathe so well, and they had to leave.

For some physical empaths things can get so bad they end up being ill for years. Dealing with big crowds, other people's stress, anger and pain can drain them a lot. Physical empaths (who are not yet empowered and in control of their sensitivities) do not have the defenses that others have to screen or filter things out, and that's why it's so crucial to self-check to see if you are one. Trust me, this can be a revelation that changes everything in your world, it certainly changed mine. If you do identify with this type of empath, trust me you are not crazy, there's nothing wrong with you, and you are definitely not a hypochondriac or malingerer. What you are is a really sensitive and gifted empath. The more you learn how to manage, protect and harness your unique way of being the more you can thrive.

Psychometric Empath

This type of empath has a unique ability to receive energy, memories and significant information from physical objects. This can be clothing, photographs, jewelry or any other type of physical object. If you realize that when you touch or come into contact with a physical object some new information streams into your consciousness, then you could very well be a psychometric empath. The more you develop this into a skill, the more powerful it becomes. You can also detect if there is any "dark" presence or energy in things.

Precognitive Empath

This type of empath has the power to receive visions about the future and can foretell an upcoming event. He or she can glance at something that isn't yet manifested and predict it accurately. If this is one of your unique abilities, then you've probably experienced events in your dreams, which then come to pass. Usually, your information is passed on while you dream or meditate. You can either receive signals relevant to some future events or see exactly what's going to happen.

Geomantic empath

A geomantic empath also called an environmental empath has the ability to connect to the physical landscape of a place. If you are this type of empath, then you've probably found yourself feeling unhappy or uncomfortable in certain places, and you couldn't logically explain why. On the contrast, you might feel drawn to certain places and experience a deep connection to places you've never even been to before. You also tend to be attracted to churches, sacred stones, groves or other areas of divine power. It's easy for you to pick up on the energy of a place or location and can be able to sense joy, fear sadness or any other dormant energetic presence that a place has. Similar to earth empath, you feel a powerful connection to the natural world and being out in nature is the best way for you to recharge. Developing this natural connection to the natural surroundings around you could lead to very intriguing opportunities so do your best to connect more with this aspect of yourself and surround yourself with natural materials as much as possible.

Animal Empath

An animal empath has a special connection with animals. He or she can feel what it's like to be that animal and one can even observe a particular communication or exchange happening between the empath and the animal. If this is you, then you'll notice that animals are very drawn to you. As you learn to develop this gift, you'll be able to help pets and their owners, and it won't be too hard to make a killer living working with animals.

For example, I read a story on Facebook of a girl who was sharing how she's managed to create a six-figure business just from dog walking. Well, it first started as a dog-walking job. She needed to make money fast after completing her degree but was struggling to find work and pay off student loans. Then someone recommended she offer some dog walking services around the neighborhood since everyone knew how much pets loved her. Within three months of starting she was already overbooked. Then she had the brilliant idea of leveraging her newly acquired design skills to create animal accessories and sell them to her clients and via Facebook. Three years in and her business is now making six figures in annual revenue. Talk about sharing your light with the world. She's happy, doing what she loves and making a lot of animals really happy. I even read a testimonial of an old lady that said she hires this girl to accompany them to the vet because her dog is always more calm and receptive to the doctor when the dog sitter is around. Booking her for such things now costs hundreds of dollars, which the dog owners consider money well spent. That's the power of using your light to design a life you love living.

Am I an empath?

If you've been questioning whether or not you are an empath, especially since you found out there is such a thing, the best way to get answers is through self-reflection. By taking the time to go within and ask yourself a few questions, you'll be able to tell whether there's resonance with the attributes and traits that most empaths possess.

I am sure you're highly intuitive; as such I trust you'll allow this process to be as natural and resistance free as possible. When something feels right and true for you, it probably is. When it doesn't, then don't force yourself to fit in just for the sake of it. You might find that some of the questions I share below don't resonate and that's okay.

It's also possible to find other teachers saying empaths are introverted and perhaps you are social and extroverted. That doesn't mean you're not an empath, it just means you are unique. As a one of a kind human being, trying to fit into one perfect category is still falling short of expressing who you really are. Therefore regardless of how well you identify with these standard questions, know that you will most likely express your empathic abilities in your own uncommon way. Answer the following questions inspired by Dr. Judith Orloff's self-assessment test. If you strongly agree the answer will be yes. Strongly disagree with a no.

1. When you walk into a room, you can always pick up the "energy" or vibe of the place.
2. You always tell very quickly if someone says one thing but means another.
3. Your mood shifts depending on who walks into the room.
4. Large crowds usually overwhelm you.
5. You feel drained after being around certain people for too long.

6. Being around certain people makes you feel sick.

7. You often feel the pain or discomfort of other people and animals.

8. People usually come to you when they have a problem.

9. The energy of the ocean, forest, mountain or nature, in general, is preferable to the city.

10. You have to be near water.

11. Violent media is a huge turn off for you because you get physically or emotionally ill when exposed to it.

12. You notice you can influence the moods of those around you.

13. Often you can't tell if you're feeling your own emotions or someone else's.

14. Anxiety and overwhelm are common occurrences for you.

15. Multitasking or taking on too much at once is an energy drainer, and you prefer to do one thing at a time.

16. You prefer one-to-one interactions or small intimate groups but certainly not large gatherings.

17. Intimate relationships are great, but you worry they will suffocate you.

18. You often feel like you don't "fit in."

19. Yelling, conflict, and fighting make you sick.

The more agreement you make with these statements, the more you would be considered a full-blown empath. If you responded yes to at least five of these statements, then we would consider you partially an empath.

Answering yes to fifty percent of these statements means you have strong empathic tendencies and of course if you answer yes to over sixty percent then welcome to the world of living as a full-blown empath. In the following chapters, I show you how to get empowered and thrive.

Chapter 02: The Game Of Energy

One of the biggest revelations this book can give you is that of recognizing that you are playing the game of energy. Everything around us vibrates, and we as empaths have naturally been gifted with the ability to sense those vibrations and even embody them. So when we recognize an energy pattern in or around us that doesn't empower and uplift us, it is our duty to quickly dissolve and transform that energy first within our bodies and if possible extend it outwardly to others as well.

I believe empaths have the power to bring about healing and high frequency energies that can literally heal people, animals, and our planet. But we cannot give what we have not got so before we talk about using our gifts and powers to help others we must first master helping ourselves.

Embracing The Empathic Experience

Most empaths confess that they just don't feel like they fit in. They go their whole lives trying to blend in and stay under the radar, even as their emotional discomfort and restlessness continue to pile on. For many empaths, their unique abilities and sensitivities go unappreciated. This is true by normal societal measures because we live on a planet that is very focused on competition, material accomplishments, getting ahead, resenting each other and so on. This is a very different perspective from the one held by an empath. If we grow up in an environment that doesn't embrace our uniqueness then often a conflict emerges within us because we constantly feel lost, misunderstood and unappreciated. The burden of having to carry around our unresolved conflicts as well as the sensitivity to other people's emotions (whether they are aware of their own emotions or not) can be a daunting task, and I think that's where many of us struggle. Coping with daily life as an empath in a world that is insensitive is not easy. Trying to explain to someone who has lost touch with their own emotions what it's like to be me is almost impossible. They will call me strange, abnormal, weird and weak. If I make the mistake (which I did in the past) of believing their opinion, then I imprison myself falsely, and life becomes almost unbearable.

I read an article on the Internet shared by an empath called Zoey who was confessing how tough things have been for her over the past twenty-six years. She recently discovered that she's an empath and that there are many of us in the world which finally gave her the peace and sense of belonging she's been searching for. "I used to dream about shapes and music, and the feelings that went along with different shapes. Trying to explain the color green to a non-empath is a lot easier than trying to explain what a shape feels like. Trust me, not only do they think you're extremely odd, but someone once asked me if I smoke an illegal substance."

There are many more who could share similar frustrations as they try to fit in where they don't. The only path of freedom for us as empaths is to step into our power, recognize that it's not about fitting into society. It's about mastering the unique gifts we bring to the table and gathering more with those that get us. The way we feel, see, experience and express ourselves is different and that's not something to be ashamed of. Who you are is what you need to learn to celebrate and boldly demonstrate in the world. Your job now is to find your truth and unique abilities and live that truth. Use your unique gifts and skills to bring to life the conditions and experiences that you've always dreamed of. The more you do, the more impactful and enjoyable your life becomes.

The Painful Struggle Of Emotional Imbalance

Before your life can go from burdensome, constricting and draining to magnificent, you'll have to come to grips with the same truth I had to face. Nothing changes unless you change first.

The main change you'll have to make is taking full ownership of your energy and learning to distinguish when you're experiencing your own emotions and when it is that of another. Discord within you is an indicator that something is out of whack and everything will continue to be a painful struggle unless you learn to replace emotional discord with harmony. You must gain mastery over your emotions and learn to handle your sensitivities. This is the difference between empowered empaths and disempowered empaths. The way to move from victimhood and feeling like this is a curse begins with a conscious decision. Choose to work on understanding your emotions and abilities.

Chances are you go through life feeling like the weight of the world is on your shoulders. You see the depths of the world's problems and feel the hurt, pain, and confusion that's being caused by greed, injustice, and war. You're also keenly aware of the heavy stuff that people tend to dump on you whenever they turn to you for relief from their issues. There's no way around this. I'm not going to tell you that it's easy living in our current world as an empath. But just because it's challenging doesn't mean it should be unbearable. There are two choices you have once you discover that you are an empath. The first choice is carrying on as you were - feeling the angst, discord, and stress of having these abilities. This is the victim state. Feeling sorry for yourself, wondering why this is happening to you and hating your life doesn't change the fact that you are still alive and walking this human journey. You will continue to create conditions and life experience even if you choose to spend the rest of your days in bed under covers. The second choice you have is to reap the benefits of having these abilities. It's about stepping into your power and learning to make empathy work for you, so you don't become a victim to other people's emotions and thought processes. It's also about learning to take care of yourself more and putting your needs first. That's a tough one for empaths, I know. And I've devoted a section on self-care tips that I'm sure will help you a lot.

Once you decide to become an empowered empath, the next step in ending the struggle and suffering is to understand what emotions are and how they help shape your reality.

So what are emotions?
An emotion is a thought linked to a sensation. A thought is in the mind, and the sensation is in the body, that's why we call our emotions

feelings. The mind is an embodied (in the body) and relational process that regulates the flow of energy and information in our body. I learned this definition from Deepak Chopra, and it has served me well over the years because it gives me a scientific and practical way of understanding what my emotions are and how they affect and shape my reality. It also helps me realize that the bigger game I am playing as a gifted empath is that of Energy. Learning how to harness, read, sense and transmute energy into anything I desire better than most.

Dr. Chopra also teaches that there are two basic types of emotions. Emotions that connect us to life. They include love, kindness, joy, compassion, gratitude, and equanimity. Then there are emotions that alienate us from life. They include fear, resentment, hostility, greed, jealousy, anger, guilt, shame, and depression. All these emotions are mediated by the part of our brain called the limbic system. All self-regulation and what is known as homeostasis takes place in this part of our brain. Since we now realize that the limbic brain is also the seat of emotions, our experience of life and whether we create an experience of great joy or great suffering will depend greatly on whether we dwell on negative emotions or positive ones. Peace and harmony in your outer world is, therefore, a direct expression of your inner emotional state. Now, for most people, creating a relatively calm internal state is easier since they don't go around receiving all the surrounding energies. But for empaths, it takes a conscious effort on our part to maintain control of our inner state. In other words, if we are so exposed to an insensitive, greedy, hate-filled and fearful environment, we tend to soak up more of that frequency which only devastates our well-being and state of mind. As a result, we shape our reality accordingly and end up struggling, suffering from depression anxiety and so on. The more aware we become of who we are, how our mind works and the energies we entertain in our inner world, the more power we'll have to end struggle and imbalance within. Over time, we are then able to not only create inner harmony, but we can also influence our immediate surrounding and others.

Are you starting to see the tremendous power you possess as an empath?

The Five Areas Of Active Expression

We have just discovered that your outer world is a reflection of your inner world. When this first hit me, all I wanted to do is start fixing some of the areas that were not working for me. Mainly my relationships, health, and finances. Can you relate?

If you've been feeling stuck lately and you believe you'll never find a way out, the negative emotions associated with your beliefs will reinforce the way you see yourself in the world, and every area of your life shall reflect the same. There are five main areas that I think empaths really need help with. Health, relationships, finances, spiritual, and career. By properly utilizing the gifts we've been given we can actually use our emotions to inform and enhance these four areas rather than hinder them. So here's a simple solution to experiment with right now.

1. Take a private journal and write down what you would love to experience and have as your daily reality in each of these areas.

Health.

Finances.

Relationships.

Career/business.

Spiritual growth.

Make sure each section gets a full page where you describe with as much color as you can the future conditions that you wish to manifest.

2. Now contrast that with where you are and notice how you interpret your current experiences. One of the biggest stumbling blocks we face is that there's so much negatively charged energy in the atmosphere, we tend to pick up on the negatives first. Some psychologists say this is due to our programming while others will say it's just because we are hanging out with the wrong people. Regardless of origin, choose to change your perception about your life, your capabilities, and your potential. Interpretations are your way of assigning meaning to the events and experiences in your life. This is how you "make meaning" out of the things that are happening to you. Empowering interpretations will help you discover the lessons or blessings in every situation, and they will enable you to move forward in life. Empowering interpretations position you to become an empowered empath. As you may have guessed, disempowering interpretations do the opposite. They will cause you to repeat

that same cycle of victimhood and being taken advantage of.

In truth, none of the interpretations you choose are any more or less real than another. Your interpretation of your life and who you are is very real to you, and you always have the power to choose the meanings you assign to your circumstances and experiences in life. You may want to interpret the last few years of your life as a curse or a blessing. You may choose to see the progress you're making in reaching your goals, or you can label yourself a failure. The relationships in your life whether positive or negative can either be helping you become a better version of yourself or a severe source of pain. I encourage you to start viewing yourself as a gifted and powerful individual. Someone with untapped potential that's seeking expression in the physical world. The more you choose to focus on how you can create the love life, career, health, family life, and fulfillment you desire instead of focusing on why it can't be, the more positivity you'll begin to experience.

Now that you know what you want in all the areas of your life that matter to you, let's share a few tips on how you can harness the power of your emotions and your unique abilities.

Harnessing the power of your emotions

Did you know that it is just as essential to process your emotions as it is to process the food you eat? We are always picking up on other people's feelings and oftentimes we just blindly absorb and let these emotions camp in our bodies. When we fail to process emotions and experiences, we create toxins similar to the way a body produces toxins, which lead to illnesses when it doesn't process food properly. But the kind of toxins we create are emotional. Anxiety, rage, guilt, sadness, hopelessness, depression and so on are all manifestations of emotional toxins. Over time, if left unchecked they morph into physical symptoms and ultimately become diseases. Having come this far into the book, it's time we start equipping you with some ways of harnessing your healthy emotions so you can slowly learn to maintain inner harmony regardless of the emotions you get exposed to.

- Take responsibility for your feelings. The most important thing you need to recognize at this point is that you have control over your emotions and sensitivities. Disempowered empaths end up being victims in life because they don't feel like they have control over their unique gifts or the emotions that dominate their lives. But the truth is, you always have the power of choice. And with this comes the ability to determine how you will respond or react at any given moment. There is nothing wrong with picking up on someone's negative energy or even landing on your own negative tendencies. Where trouble blooms is when you accept, embody and dwell in that negativity. The first step to thriving as an empath is to take complete ownership of what you feel and the gifts you've been given.

• Deal with emotions as they come up.
Since you are naturally going to pick up on the energy around you, it's best to get into the habit of discerning the emotions that dominate your day and deal with them as soon as they show up. Identify the feeling that you're experiencing, do some breath work to bring yourself more into the present moment, and then name it to tame it. Are you feeling sad, anxious, resentful, overwhelmed, jealous? Where in your body are you feeling this emotion? Ask yourself if these feelings are yours, if they've been triggered by something or if they belong to someone else? Try to figure out why you're reacting in this way and question if there is a better way to react? This doesn't mean you judge yourself. I want you to

become your very own private investigator so you can start to understand your triggers.

As you do your breathing and answer these questions, pay attention to the physical manifestation in your body especially where you're experiencing the most discomfort. Keep doing this until you notice the discomfort dissolving.

• Learn to discern when it's your emotions and when it's someone else's.

If you realized that you were reacting to someone else's energetic frequency, collect those emotions into one area and see them dissolving and flowing out from you. Refuse to be a dumping place for other people's unresolved emotions.

• Be process-oriented rather than goal oriented. As empaths, we play to a different tune. That's why most of the commonly preached personal development stuff does very little to help us thrive. Instead of chasing after goals and holding yourself to rigid standards, focus on growing, learning, thriving and showing up as your best self. Give yourself the necessary time and space to create a life you love living. As you move toward your vision, embrace the process. Take note of the day-to-day changes as you progress. Be more mindful of triggers that set you off and respect your sensitivities. Celebrate yourself and this journey even if you're not going at the same pace as others because your journey is unique and no one can tell you what success should look like. Take the time to redefine what some of these labels mean to you in a way that empowers you.

How To Stop Being A Human Sponge

Finding the balance between exercising your empathic abilities and controlling the energies and emotions you pick from others is not an easy task. It's not uncommon for other people's vibes to have an impact on your energy level, emotional state and therefore your life experience. This goes for both good and bad vibes. The more you're surrounded by high-frequency individuals, the more those vibes influence your own reality, and the same is true if you're surrounded by low-frequency individuals. Here's the thing, I haven't yet found a magical single bullet that I can give you to help solve this issue. I also don't have a magic armor that you can wear which can make you instantly impermeable to other people's negativity. But having walked this path I have found a few tips that have gradually helped me develop the skill of being able to filter out, block or instantly process emotions that are detrimental to me.

In other words, I stopped trying to fight my powers, and I stopped judging myself for being so perceptible and sensitive to my environment. Instead, I've learned to embrace all that I am and strengthen myself so that I know the right time to take in and the right time not to. And during those times when I get hit with people's stuff, and I'm completely unprepared, I also know how to process those turbulent emotions, so I don't end up drained and unwell. Here's a fast way of processing negative vibes when they unexpectedly hit.

- Ground yourself.
- Create some distance between you and the negative energy. Whether physically or mentally depending on the situation.
- Personal discernment. Figure out if it's you being triggered. Maybe it's something within you that the other person is triggering. If it is, take note and work on it once you're out of that situation.
- Practice tuning out especially when in the presence of energy vampires.
- Find a technique that works for you that helps you rejuvenate and clears your energy. I like using music because it quickly sends me to my happy place so I can instantly shift back to high vibes before continuing with the rest of

my day. Some people prefer praying, meditating or lighting incense. Pick whatever works for you. The main thing is being able to notice what's happening within you and taking quick action before it escalates into something big.

There are more techniques and practices that I will be sharing in upcoming chapters but keep these quick tips as your go-to hacks whenever you need fast relief.

Chapter 03: Relationships

In the previous chapter, I made you aware of the fact that this is a game of energy and self-mastery. To thrive as empaths in today's world, we need awareness about who we truly are and how to make the most of the unique abilities we possess.

In relationships, this becomes all the more important because where two people are exchanging energy, things can get quite constricting and draining for an empath even when that's not the main intention. Your highly sensitive nature and ability to pick up on the energetic frequencies surrounding you makes every relationship quite challenging whether it is romantic, familial or work-related. The closer you connect with someone, the more vulnerable you are to the emotions they radiate and the more you can feel what they are going through mentally, emotionally and physically. If you already work as a healer or during times when you are engaged in sexual intercourse with a partner you know how vulnerable those moments are for you because the energy of another fully penetrates and blends with your own. It is due to this fact that many empaths including myself find handling relationships a very challenging task. We love being affectionate, offering our support, giving of ourselves wholeheartedly but we also know how overwhelming and constricting that constant giving can be.

I struggled to stay in a long-term relationship for most of my adult life because I would always feel in bondage to my partner after a while even if I loved them. Interacting with the same person so much would cause me to feel suffocated and exhausted because I didn't feel like I was getting enough quiet and alone time to replenish my energy. There is a deep desire within me to be alone that constantly battles with my strong passion for love, and although I cannot say I've completely resolved it, I have found a way to create some harmony. Many of the tips I use to create thriving relationships I share in this chapter. Since I know some empaths are also raising children, I have also dedicated a small section of this chapter to discussing how we can manifest better relationships with our children. I'm going to share with you a few lessons I've learned about being an empath in an intimate relationship and how to make it work especially if it's with a non-empath. But before we get there, something I want to address is the struggle and suffering that most of us face.

Why you've struggled, suffered from loneliness and felt misunderstood all your life.

Here's the thing no one wants to talk about. No "right lover" will come into your life and make everything perfect in your world. If you have unresolved issues, wounds that need healing and emotional turbulence, it doesn't really matter who walks into your life, you still won't experience your happily ever after. As long as you're stuck in the frequency of suffering and loneliness, everything you experience will continue to match that frequency. You'll be more prone to attracting people that only solidify that reality. It is easy to become embroiled in an unhealthy and dysfunctional relationship with someone who has strong traits associated with narcissism when one is stuck in a state of struggle and suffering.

Another blind spot we tend to have comes from our natural healing abilities. We get drawn to people who are emotionally wounded and struggling, and those in need of healing of some kind are also drawn to us, but usually, such relationships typically don't end well. This is where codependency comes in. If you are in a relationship with someone who depends on you to heal their wounds or validate them you also unknowingly attach a feeling of worthiness to that person because you know they depend on you for survival.

Being overly invested in the well being of someone you love can lead to great suffering, and it's essential you become aware of the blind spots you have. The intention you need to have as you approach any relationship is to find that overlap between being your best self and loving someone else.

Do any of these experiences ring true for you?
• Arguments make me ill or sick.
• I have difficulty setting boundaries and asserting my needs.
• I absorb my partner's stress, symptoms, and emotions.
• I'm afraid of losing my own identity in a relationship.
• I need to be along to refuel and recharge.

Empaths and intimacy

Intimacy is a big one for us. This is true whether you are dating a fellow empath or a non-empath. We are known as passionate human beings and for a good reason. Our experience of everything is usually pretty intense. We feel everything and everyone, and when it comes to loving someone, we love hard. During the "honeymoon" phase when you just start dating someone things are incredible. It's only as you get deeper into each other, spend more time and open yourself up fully (all the time) to your partner that things start going awry for you. Intimacy in relationships can be fun for you too especially as you learn to step into your full power, manage your sensitivities and attract only the ideal relationships.

Being loved by an empath is one of the most wonderful experience for anyone to go through. However, not many people are prepared for this kind of intense relationship. The contrast of going from intense togetherness to complete space and time alone is a bit of a conundrum and takes a certain type of mindset to fully comprehend why being together and being apart is equally important. And it is that kind of person you should focus on attracting into your life. But you can only attract someone new if you become someone new.

How to manifest your dream relationships

I said it in the last statement. If you want to manifest relationships that nourish and excite you, there must be a fundamental shift in you first. I once read a quote somewhere of a conversation between a father and son. The son asked his father, " How do I find the right woman?" The father replied, "don't worry about finding the right woman just focus on becoming the right man."

It's the perfect mindset for you and me to carry into our lives as well. When I stopped looking for the perfect soul mate and instead placed all my attention of healing my energy, taking control of my emotions, grounding myself and becoming the best version of myself that I could be, that's when things took a major turn in my life. Here's the tough pill you need to swallow. You won't find your ideal soul mate until you become a perfect match for him or her. So what does an ideal relationship entail?

It's about physical attraction and strong natural chemistry.
When you're with your soul mate you feel a shared mutual love and connection, you're comfortable and safe.

It's about being each other's biggest fans and becoming emotional mirrors and teachers.

Your soul mate will "get you," and whenever conflict arises, you will be able to work through them and relinquish unhealthy patterns to improve the relationship.

What it doesn't entail is the following:
One-sided. Meaning it's all about you or all about your partner.
It's also not just a superficial physical attraction where only the sex is good.

A soulful relationship doesn't include abuse, control, rigidity or taking advantage of each other in any way.

It's also not about convenience or just settling down out of fear of being alone. Sometimes a soul mate relationship lasts a lifetime, other times they don't, but regardless, these relationships are transformative and always teach us a lot.

I finally met the love of my life. And even though I still work hard to find that balance between my desire to be in this relationship and my desire to be alone, I can genuinely say the relationship has never been better. If you are in a relationship and want to take it to the next level or if you're still on the quest of finding your soul mate, here's what I recommend.

• Begin by creating a vision of what your ideal relationship should look like. Identify the qualities you want your soul mate to have. Ask yourself: What would feel so good to me? What do I need? Someone who is kind, spiritually connected, supportive, reliable and generous? Does he or she also want children? The more clarity you have on what qualities you desire, the easier it becomes to attract them into your life.

• Once you have clarity, you must embody those same qualities. And with that embodiment (where you are doing the inner work to become the ideal soul mate for them), you also learn to surrender, trust in the process of life and build the right expectation that as you continue to become this new you, they are moving closer toward you.

• Listen to your intuition as you go about your daily life and notice what you intuitively feel as you interact with new people. If you meet someone, do you feel a sudden wave of chills, a gut feeling of attraction or a flash of insight that you need to speak with this person? Or do you get a stomach cramp, feel sick or distrustful? These are all signals that are meant to keep you on the path of manifesting your ideal relationship.

• Train yourself to let go of shame. This is something many empaths have to continually work on although, to be honest, I think shame is something everyone in society has to deal with. We struggle with sexuality and intimacy when we fail to view our entire bodies as luminous and lovemaking as something sacred. The words Vagina, Penis, and sex evoke a sense of embarrassment and shame for a lot of people. I want to encourage you to see your body with enlightened eyes. Respect your particular aesthetic sensibilities and examine the ones that bring out the feeling of shame in you. Work on this in preparation for your new relationship so that as you manifest your new romance, you can be in a position to awaken sexually and use your intuition to deepen your sexual connection.

Toxic relationships and energy vampires

Sometimes you'll find yourself in a group or engaged in a conversation that almost makes you ill. These types of human interactions often drain your energy; leave you feeling low, offended, unworthy and at times even fearful. It's imperative you recognize the people in your life who uplift you and those that bring you down. Being a sponge to all that's happening around you means you cannot afford to hang out with toxic people or people who love taking advantage of you. Unfortunately, this can be a family member, client, teacher, neighbor, colleague, boss, childhood friend, lover or a strange that sat next to you on the plane. The common name given to such toxic people is "energy vampire" because they seem to suck the life out of you. There are various types of energy vampires. The jealous bees who struggle to feel happy for anyone else, the insecure ones that like to put you and others down to their level of low self-esteem. You know what I mean? They are almost like bullies. Then there are the whiners, the gossipers, the drama queens and so on. I could probably fill up this entire page with this list, but you get the point. The fact of the matter is these types of people are always looking to latch on and feed off others because they have no life force of their own to sustain them. No doubt you've met this group especially because they tend to gravitate toward disempowered empaths because they can sense they will be heard. Now, I'm not here to judge or make anyone wrong, but I do know that you need to steer clear of these people if you want to thrive.

As we get more and more exposed to such people, we soak in that same frequency, and those negative emotions create lots of turbulence within. Dr. Judith Orloff wrote in her book that energy vampires do more than drain your physical energy. The super-malignant ones can make you believe you're an unworthy, unlovable wretch who doesn't deserve any better. She also shares some signs that we need to look out for in her Emotional Freedom book.

Your eyelids get heavy as though you're ready for a nap.
Your mood takes a nosedive.
You want to binge on carbs and other comfort foods.

You feel anxious, depressed or negative even though you don't know why.

You feel put down, sniped at or slimed. Whenever you start to notice any of these changes taking place within you, there's probably an energy vampire around you looking to destabilize your emotional center.

About a year ago one of my close friends started dating a man that seemed very charming. She was definitely smitten and couldn't stop talking about him when they first met. A few weeks into it she started complaining that every time she spends a weekend at his place she usually comes back home feeling more tired than usual. I recommended she paid more attention to what was happening in her body while they were spending time together. That's when she started being mindful of what was happening inside her. After a week of continued self-observation, she realized each time they would meet to go out, she would come back home with a migraine. She assumed it must be her old migraine trying to creep back into her life, but I insisted she takes the time to investigate if there was a connection between her discomforts and this new relationship.

Underneath all the attraction and charm she was experiencing, this guy was certainly not good for her overall wellbeing. It took a while for her to realize he was actually a strong narcissist because somehow she would mute out her intuition whenever he was around but then suffer the consequences later. It was as if she was under a spell. The relationship only lasted a few months because as much as she loved having fun and being reckless with him, she was really struggling with her health and inner peace. Sometimes we find ourselves caught up in this complex situation where the person we care about is just no good for us. The best outcome for everyone concerned is always to walk away.

Protecting yourself from toxic relationships.

It's only natural that I share some prescriptions that can help empower you as you go through your day because we all know there will always be those that we cannot avoid interacting with who aren't good for our well being. Besides, as we move about in society, it's important to make sure we are able to keep off the energetic frequencies that do not serve us and attract more of those that do. Here are some ways you can do that.

• Ground yourself several times throughout the day.

This is best done barefoot and can be as long or as short as you like. You might choose to ground yourself in the morning before engaging with anyone and then do quick short ones throughout the day. The purpose of this technique is to bring yourself back into the present moment, step into your full power and then deal with other people from a position of strength.

Here's how to do it if faced with a stressful situation: Focus on your senses and become aware of your surroundings. Shift your focus from the stressful person and transfer your attention to any soothing sound that you hear blocking out everything else.

• Practice deep breathing before beginning an interaction with someone. Breath control is a highly effective method to bring yourself back into a point of power and can be done instantly. Simply breathe in deeply at intervals for a few minutes until you notice a calming presence taking over your mind and emotions. The more you practice this as you interact with people, the better you'll get at stabilizing your emotions in real time whenever you need it.

- Learn to recognize the type of energy vampire you're having to deal with and protect yourself accordingly.

If for example, you find yourself in the company of a narcissist, realize this person is emotionally limited. Don't make yourself prey to their opinions by attaching your identity or self-worth to them. If interacting with such a person is unavoidable then do your best to communicate with them in a manner that resonates with them and helps them see what's in it for them.

On the other hand, if you're dealing with a borderline personality, the best thing you can do is to stay calm. Practice self-control and avoid reacting just because they push your buttons. Knowing that these types of people feed off anger and enjoy pitting people against each other step away before they include you in rants and anger fest. Refuse to take sides, set clear structures, be firm and let them know your boundaries.

- Find your inner harmony.

Instead of allowing the environment to affect your mood, train your mind and body to find the source of stability within yourself.

- Shield yourself by imagining some shape around your body and aura that keeps you safe from outside energies.

This shield is made of white light that's meant to protect you from any negativity. Now, I will tell you that this is one of the most recommended tactics by many teachers of this topic; however, I don't think it's the best solution. By locking yourself inside your bubble of light, nothing comes in, but nothing flows either. And as you protect yourself from energies, even good energy doesn't come in. In other words, I see it as building up a big wall; sure it keeps the bad guys out, but it also keeps out the good ones.

This might be a great technique to apply when you're just starting out and working on self-mastery but as you learn to handle your sensitivities I encourage you to find techniques that resonate with you which also promote the flow of good energy.

• Find time to be in nature.

For most empaths, nature is the best healer. Whether that's walking on the grass barefoot, on a sandy beach, hugging a tree or whatever else resonates with you. Do this regularly and especially after being exposed to energy vampires so that you can replenish and cleanse your energy.

Parenting

Empathic parents often think there's something wrong with them especially if they don't know of their unique gifts. Relationships, in general, are a challenge, but when you become a parent, it takes things to a whole new level. If you are a parent, this section here is going to help you and those you're raising. But if you're not yet playing the parental role, I suggest skipping over to the next chapter because we are about to jump into the deep end of the struggles that come with being an empath and a parent.

Others might think your overreact or struggle from anxiety problems because of how overwhelmed and burned out you are. While other parents are chilled and barely give their kids a second glance when out and about, you probably spend every minute tracking their every move. You're so attuned to your child that even the slightest change in their mood immediately affects you. When your child falls, you cringe. If she hurts herself or comes home after a bad day at school, you can literally feel her pain. When she has a stomach upset or catches the flu the experience is often more unbearable to you than it is to her. This is a common experience for every empathic parent I know so don't worry, you are not alone, and there's nothing wrong with you.

A recent study showed that children of highly empathic parents thrive and are psychologically and physically healthier, happier and more balanced. I can easily see why that is. Empathic parents create an atmosphere of love, giving, compassion, safety, peace and they are so attuned to their children it's only natural a child will grow up well nurtured. On the other hand, the same study revealed that empathic parents (as great as they are) need to be on the lookout for stress-related problems. Empathic parents tend to have higher inflammation levels because they are always concerned and hyper-vigilant. Being overly cautious and alert is very taxing to your body which as we know becomes detrimental long-term. Being a caring nurturing and thoughtful parent is great, but you must pay attention to your tendencies of going overboard and putting the best interests of others before your own. Yes, I know this is your child, but even so, you still need to tend to your individual needs first unless you want to end up burned out and chronically fatigued.

I want to encourage you to find harmony and create a system of nurturing that works for you and your child. To do this, there are a few practical things you can begin doing today.

• Cultivate emotional resilience.
Learn to detach from what your child is feeling so that you don't feel it so intensely. And yes, there's nothing wrong with detaching from your child's intense emotions from time to time because it helps calm your mind and give you the right perspective. Train your emotions to be less reactive whenever something happens to your child.

• Be more kind to yourself.
Seek to completely eradicate self-criticism, comparing yourself with other parents or judging how you react to situations. Use a kind

tone and speak kindly to yourself whenever you carry out an inner dialogue.

• Prioritize some alone time regularly so you can refuel.

All empaths need time alone to unwind and rejuvenate, but I know things get tough once you become a parent. The only time you have alone might be during bathroom breaks, and you know what, if that's all you can get, then make the most of it. Schedule a specific time of the day where your "bathroom break" is actually an alone time where you can just be with yourself. Of course, if you can engage in some activity that helps you refuel like taking a long salt bath, walking in nature, reading a book, praying or whatever gets you in the zone, then, by all means, do it regularly.

• Learn to create distance whenever you feel emotional imbalance creeping in.

Unless you want to constantly spiral into anxiety or get stuck in a foul mood that seems to come from nowhere, I recommend you get into the habit of taking a step back and allowing your emotions to process when you get triggered. Analyze your emotions, find the source of negativity and release them.

• Set clear boundaries for everyone in the family including your child.
You need to teach your child what healthy boundaries in your family set-up look like. This isn't going to be easy because sooner or later your child will realize other kids have it differently and it may raise some comparison issues. This is where you'll have to be firm, loving and creative with how things run in your home. Find a middle ground that works for both you and the child especially if they are old enough to carry personal preferences as well.

• Ban any and all emotional drama.
Empaths cannot handle emotional tension, yelling, and conflict very well. We also cannot thrive around negativity. As such, it is

imperative that you teach your child the difference between negative and positive emotions as early on as possible. Help them understand the importance of communicating honestly, peacefully and thoughtfully. Show them how to practice self-control and how to avoid the common trap of emotional selfishness.

• Take it one day at a time.
Being a parent is a hard job for anyone. Add in our empathic sensitivities and tendencies to seek solitude, and the challenge quadruples. You will be challenged a lot but the reward will be even greater, and the stronger your connection and understanding with your child, the more enjoyable the journey will be.

The more you can take care of yourself and build up your emotional resilience the more you will have to give to your family. Now, what if you're raising an empathic child?

Raising empathic children

In our highly insensitive society, it's your job as a parent to recognize if your child is an empath. Empathic children have nervous systems that rapidly react to strong external stimuli including stress. They feel too much and frequently don't know how to manage this sensory overload. The main problem is that the children can't yet articulate what they are experiencing. This was one of the main issues I faced growing up. I realized that I see more, hear more, smell more and experience more emotions than the other kids around me. I was highly intuitive at a very young age and could tell when my parents were fighting even if I didn't hear them doing it. I could tell when something was wrong with my teacher even when she was trying hard to act normal in class. Strong smells, bright lights, and loud talking really affected me, and I preferred to be on my own or with a few close friends. Most people in school called me shy, weak and antisocial.

In fact, I can recall one time in 4th grade during playtime we had a substitute teacher who found it very odd that I was sitting in class blissfully coloring my favorite mandala. He called me over and asked me if there was something wrong with me. "No," I responded with a smile. He wanted to know if the other kids were refusing to play with me or if I was hurt by something. When I told him I was just enjoying my coloring session, he looked puzzled. So just to ease his discomfort, I decided to spend a few minutes outside playing with the other kids. It's tough to be an empathic child in a world that misjudges your behavior and tries to force you to fit in with the other kids. But empathic children can never fit in and when we force them to do things they aren't comfortable with we trigger unnecessary stress and negative emotional experiences.

As a parent, you need to discern as early on as possible whether you have an empathic child or not because as I said, they won't be able to tell you. Some signs to look out for include:

Your child gets overwhelmed really quickly. Both stimuli and school always overwhelm him or her. If you're out in a mall or a big party, your child will choose to cling on to you and stay by your side. You'll notice they are experiencing every smell, all the loud voices, and sounds around them. When the teacher yells or gives too much homework, they will come home completely distraught and feeling defeated.

Try this:
Get to know the triggers that destabilize your child and help to reduce them as much as possible. Have a word with the teachers if you need to and perhaps don't take them into the mall when it's busiest.

- You'll notice your child cries when others around them are hurt or upset. If you see an ad on TV showing how children are dying from lack of water and food and your child immediately falls apart, he or she is probably an empath. You might also have noticed they get sobby whenever there's a family feud at home or if one of their friends gets mad, hurt or upset.

Try this:
Teach your child to be grounded and to center their own energy whenever they experience that discomfort from others. Help them distinguish when they are mirroring other people's emotions and show them how to stay in the present moment. Once your child learns to be calm in an uncomfortable situation praise them for being kind and concerned for others and then offer a way of helping out that helps them detach. This will look different for every situation but let me share an example of something my mom taught me.

I remember a time when my best friend came to school with swollen eyes. She had been crying all night and all morning. Her parents were getting divorced, and she would be staying with her mom while her dad was moving to another state. It was tragic. Seeing her that way immediately made me sick. That day I couldn't even have lunch. We just sat next to each other in the school cafeteria in silence and barely touched our food. By the time I got home that evening I had a terrible headache, my tummy was all knotted up, and I had this heaviness in my chest that made it hard to breathe. At first, my mom thought I was catching something. She checked my fever and was about to suggest we pay the doctor's office a visit when she paused, took a deep breath in and asked me if anything strange had happened at school. I shared the whole story (in sobs) after which we just sat there in silence with her arms around me.

After what seemed like a really long time for me, she asked me if I wanted to try something that would help me feel better and also help my friend. We sat down on the carpet, clasped hands and she took me through some kind of a breathing technique. Initially, I didn't want to do it, but seeing her do it and knowing that it might help my friend somehow, I stuck with it. A few minutes later I felt very calm, and the heaviness in my chest was gone. Then she asked me, " are you feeling hurt right now?"

"I don't know," I said. She told me she was very proud of how much I care about the people around me and especially my friend. Then she explained that adults behave in strange ways sometimes and can hurt us without meaning to but, if I want to be an excellent friend I need to be strong and loving and reliable and encouraging so that my friend can find a way through this challenging phase. It totally resonated with me. The more I become a loving friend, the more she would stop feeling like all was lost. So my mom asked me if there was anything special I wanted to do for my friend to remind her of how much I love her. I immediately jumped up in excitement. "Yes. I want to bake her favorite cookies and take them to school tomorrow", I said. Mom was more than happy to help me bake and delighted me, even more, when she said that we could take them to her house before dinner time that same day. I can't tell you what a difference that single experience made in my life and I have carried on that ritual of approaching pain and hurt the same way.

Your child is unique and may require a different approach, it's up to you to find what works for you. No one in my life understood me for a big part of my life, but my mother always did. Even though she's not an empath and had no knowledge of what empaths are, she did see me as a sensitive child and did an excellent job helping me manage my sensitivities while growing up. Dr. Judith Orloff has an assessment that can help you score your child's level of sensitivity. Answer the questions below, and if you get 9-12 yesses, then your child is an extreme empath. If you get 6-9 yesses, then your child is a strong empath. 4-8 yesses indicate your child is moderate and 1-3 indicates your child possess some empathic traits.

1. Does he or she feel things deeply?
2. Does he or she get over-stimulated by people, large crowds, noise or stress?
3. Does he or she have strong reactions to sad or frightening scenes in books or movies?
4. Does he or she want to escape and hide from family gatherings because there's too much going on?
5. Does he or she feel "different" than the other kids or complain about not fitting in?
6. Is he or she a good listener and compassionate with others?
7. Does he or she have a strong connection to nature, animals, plants or stuffed animals?
8. Does he or she require a lot of time alone rather than playing with other kids?

9. Does he or she take on your own or other people's emotions or stress - and act out when you're angry upset or depressed?

10. Does he or she have one best friend and a few good friends rather than a vast social network?

Here are a few tips to help you create more of that calm, nurturing, and safe environment for your empathic child so both of you can enjoy this ride even more.

• Be an emotional coach.

Your child doesn't have the emotional vocabulary needed to communicate what they are experiencing effectively. It is your job to help them learn how to name and tame the emotions that show up. Talk openly about feelings and guide them to become emotionally literate. Find moments daily where you connect face-to-face and listen to them. Validate your child's feelings by acknowledging what you're picking up from them. When they seem sad, let them know "you seem sad, is everything okay?" Point out feelings in books, films that you watch together or people that you encounter. Use stories and emotional words to teach them things.

• Increase their self-awareness.

Make your child aware of their unique ability to feel, sense and experience everything deeply. Help him, or her discern the difference between emotions that stream out of their own consciousness and those that they pick up from other people including you. The more aware they can become, the easier it will be to gain emotional mastery and become warrior empaths as they grow.

• Create rituals for grounding.

This is one of the main things I would love every empathic child to learn even before they can write. It helps alleviate so much of the stress and suffering that they would be exposed to as they grow. I wish I had learned how to ground and center myself as a child. But hey, at least you can pass it down to your child and save them a lot of pain and heartache. The younger the child, the more you'll need to improvise but if the child is old enough, teach them the grounding method in this book as well as some of the practices I will be sharing on the chapter on self-care.

• Set a regular "decompress" time.
Your child needs time to unwind and refuel himself or herself. Make sure they have time daily to do this especially if they are already going to school and interacting with the society a lot.

• Teach them how to focus on the process and growth, not the goals.
I know it will be tempting to get your child into goal setting, beating everyone in the class and completing tasks so that teachers and others feel good. Instead, I want to encourage you to

train your child to stay on his or her own path or growth and learning. Empaths will always do things differently, and it's crucial as children they learn that the process is just as important as the achievement.

• Create an emotional container that supports your child and helps them feel safe, heard and loved.

Let your child know that they can count on you no matter what. As you do, your child will start to develop strong self-regulation skills. They will also have the courage to process emotions and be proud of their sensitivities and unique abilities. As we all know, that sense of empowerment leads to very active, happy and prosperous members of society. One cannot give what one doesn't have. Empathic children can only grow up to be influential leaders in our community if we do a good job creating a space for them where they feel good about who they are. An environment that creates security and emotional stability so that they don't have to go through life on defense mode, fighting against an invisible enemy.

• Allow your child to see your vulnerability.
This is not something you'll hear mainstream parents talking about. Most parents believe in masking their emotions in front of their children. Not that it works, but at least some manage to get away with it for a while. As a parent raising an empath, however, you don't stand a chance at success if you try to pull this off. Your child will always know what's happening with you whether you admit it or not. Instead of creating a relationship with him or her that's based on lying, why not share the journey together. It's okay for your child to see you stumble and fall in your dreams, your emotional mastery, and growth as a human being. The more you can show your child that life is about progress, not perfection and that there is strength in vulnerability, the stronger he or she will be too. Sounds counterintuitive I know, but just test it for a while. It will

strengthen your relationship and take off unnecessary pressure for you and your child.

The fact that both of you have come to enjoy this human journey as companions as miraculous and perfect enough. There's no need to "pretend" or "fake it." As I said, it's about focusing on the process and the progress, not the goals. If you genuinely believe that, then it's time you emulate it in your life. Being vulnerable doesn't have to be something extraordinary. Something as simple as apologizing to your child when you've made a mistake or sharing a lesson you've learned from interacting with someone can help develop a sense of stability and normalcy with your child.

Chapter 04: Work and Career

Job satisfaction seems to be elusive for most people on the planet. In the United States of America alone, at least fifty percent of workers report being unsatisfied and unhappy with their jobs. That's literally half the workforce. For empaths and highly sensitive individuals, that dissatisfaction runs deeper than just a paycheck and healthcare insurance. The daily challenges involved in working a regular job creates more stress than is necessary plunging most empaths deeper into that pit of despair we all need to avoid. You'll be hard pressed to go online and find anything remotely empowering about being an empath and thriving at work. Much of what you'll find are people sharing this perception that being an empath is difficult, and work is a constant struggle.

People want to take advantage of you, they might bully you, and no one ever recognizes all your dedication. We are warned that we have to be extra careful because energy vampires and narcissists at work are out to get us and prey on our abilities. Most people seem to be taking such a disempowering stand. But does it really help?

I'm not here to argue with any of these suggestions, and you know, maybe some of this information is true, but you need to be aware of the fact that your mindset and how you approach your work is what determines your experience. It is true that as an empath you will have to process and manage the energies of everyone else you work with. And that the sounds, scents, and details that most people hardly ever notice will be at the foreground for you, but that doesn't mean work should be an ongoing punishment. I want to invite you to step into a more empowering state and tell a new story about your work experience. There is a new way to be an empath and having gone through ways you can thrive in your relationships, it's time to shift focus and talk about how you can do the same when it comes to your career and business.

Being an empath is a big gift that comes with great power. With that power comes even greater responsibility and the more you learn to develop yourself the more you'll become an empowered empath. What many of us don't realize is that there are two types of empaths roaming around this planet teaching on this topic. The empowered empath who has developed himself/herself and teaches from a place of strength and self-mastery. Then there's the disempowered empath. He or she teaches from a place of victimhood and lacks the self-mastery and mental strength needed to handle his or her sensitivities. In other words, an underdeveloped empath. Depending on whose material you come across, you'll be on the receiving end of disempowering information that keeps you walking the path of struggle in your work, relationships, health, and personal fulfillment or empowering information so you can start walking the path of prosperity. I am taking a stand on being an empowered empath even at work because I know how possible it can be for all of us to thrive. I hope this book is helping you come to the same realization.

The fact that you can detect and process energy better than most people around you means that you have the power of understanding and handling work relationships better than the average person (assuming you've developed yourself). Many empaths struggle to find a job that is the right fit because they are looking for happiness in all the wrong places. As such every day feels exhausting. It is true there are overly stressful jobs that are perhaps not ideal for empaths and highly sensitive people. The amount of stimulation in such a work environment can cause a great deal of stress, overwhelm and frustration making it less ideal for the average empath but I can assure, in any "high pressure" job you could think of, I bet there exists an empath who is thriving. For example, I've met doctors, lawyers and even got to interview a military guy who is an empath. This leads me to believe that as long as you find a job that is the right fit for your unique talents and continue to develop yourself, there's no limit to where you could work. But above all else, if you want to find a job that satisfies you, the first step is to step out of a victim mindset.

Michelle, a client of mine, shared with me how unbearable life was becoming for her. We bumped into each other through a synchronistic experience when we sat together during a flight and immediately shared a connection. At the time she felt tired of the boss that was bullying her and the narcissistic colleagues that she believed were trying to manipulate and control her. The ongoing story in her mind was that she was being treated with so much hostility and that her overdue promotion had been overlooked because she's not as outspoken as the rest of the loud-mouthed personalities working with her. I pointed out that her only chance at having the life and career she wanted was to take full responsibility for her own power. She needed to stop victimizing herself and positioning her boss as the big bad wolf in her story. The reason I insisted on this is that I know nothing good can come from playing the victim. One might look for a new job, a new partner or new friends but if there's no change in mindset, even the new manifestations will turn out just as ugly.

All this is to remind you that as I share tips on how you can thrive and manifest your dream role it's important to realize that you are the determining factor. Your success and happiness at work depend primarily on your mindset, and that's where you should start making changes if you want something new. In addition to working on your mindset and choosing to become an empowered empath, I also want you to consider choosing work that aligns with your values and supports your talents. This will make the work experience way more enjoyable. Most people are choosing jobs because of pay or because "nothing else is available," which is such a disservice to their own well-being. We live in a digital age where you can be anything and work from anywhere. Whether it's a job or a business, go for something that compliments who you are as an individual. Consider the company culture you're getting into and the skills you'll need to excel and thrive in that role. I understand that we all have bills to pay, but surely you know of people who have found a way to pay bills and do work that fulfills them. Why shouldn't you have the same opportunity as well?

Recommended Jobs For Empaths.

I think any job or business can help you create your dream lifestyle as long as you've done the research. As I mentioned, even doctors can be empaths, so it isn't so much about limiting yourself to focus on a particular career. It's more about finding the right fit. And since empaths are unique individuals, there cannot be a one size fits all. Therefore, you might not resonate with any of the job suggestions I offer here, and that's okay. Use these as inspiration to help you tap into what lights you up. Experts studying and working with empaths and highly sensitive individuals put this list together. Based on their research, these jobs stand to create an environment that an empath would most likely enjoy.

- Fashion Designer.
- Interior Designer.
- Graphics Designer.
- Analyst.
- IT professional.
- Accountant.
- Animal Rescue.
- Musician.
- Actor.

- Massage therapist.
- Life coach.
- Writer.
- Artist.
- Counselor.
- Music teacher.
- Business Owner.
- Caregiver.
- Botanist.

How to manifest your dream career as an empath.

What many companies are beginning to realize is that empaths have a lot of strengths that positively impact a company's overall performance. Our ability to pay close attention, genuinely listen and understand the needs of others is integral to building a strong team. It's also a great superpower to have when serving a customer. That's why this is the best time for empaths to step up and step out boldly into the marketplace. You need to sharpen your skills, get clear on the role you want to play and reach for your dream job because I can assure you, the business world is ready to embrace leaders like you and me. If you want to build your career working for a company or on your own, here are some ideas to help you land your dream role.

• Start with your "Why."
Simon Sinek says, "people don't buy WHAT you do; they buy WHY you do it." Instead of focusing solely on what you want, I suggest you take time to figure out why you want it. Take some quiet time and journal the answer to this question: Why do you want this dream career?

I know you already have the details of your dream job outlined. But that won't be enough to help you land it. You also need clarity on why you want it so that you can clearly detect if the job interview or business niche you want to step into aligns with your values and beliefs.

- Get to know your talents and unique gifts.

Before others can learn to appreciate and value your work, they must see what you bring to the table. That implies you need to know your talents well enough to put them on the table in a way that brings value to the other person. Knowing your sensitivities, strengths, and abilities help you demonstrate to another person effortlessly. Answer these questions: What are your unique talents? What are your sensitivities? How do you see this benefiting a fellow human being?

- Understand your temperament.

If you don't know yourself and the triggers that take you off balance, it'll be hard to spot the best opportunity to cease. You need to understand the environments that help you thrive and increase your productivity so that as you go for an interview, you'll be testing to see if the working conditions will help you produce your best stuff or not. What circumstances do you feel enable you to do your best work? For example, do you enjoy working alone? In absolute silence? With music in the background? Do you feel good working with a team?

• Get your story right.

Take stock of your past experience, skills you have, all your sensitivities and gifts. Then use all these positives to direct your next career role. If you realize like the dog-walking girl, I spoke about earlier in the book that you are an animal empath and communicate naturally with all kinds of animals, use that to your advantage. It could mean you need to develop additional skills and get training to get into the medical field if that's the direction you want to go, or like her, it could be that you just need to grow a client base that trusts you. Then from there, you can start offering higher services that produce a good income. Everything depends on the story you tell yourself and how developed your talents are. Before you go hunting for your next job, do this part diligently.

• Quit idealizing this concept of "dream job for an empath."
It only leads to procrastination and unnecessary disappointment. Instead of holding this perception, focus on consciously building a lifestyle and work role that you love. Something that you do which feels meaningful to you where you make a difference in the lives of others. Create a vision for yourself and then live from that desired state. I say this because I think for many of us, this idea of a dream career or business is actually centered on a feeling of fear and lack. As strange as it may sound, most of us are trying to remedy this feeling of being different from everyone else by creating this idea that there has to be a "special" type of job for people like us. But if you think about it, people like us are here to help heal, spread light, love, and compassion in the world. I believe every industry and niche

market needs that. I would rather have a doctor who is an empath treating me instead of a non-empath. I'd rather have a hairdresser who is an empath doing my hair, and I'd undoubtedly choose an accountant who is an empath to help me understand taxes. Wouldn't you?

The key to creating a world where empaths are leaders and non-empaths learn to practice a little more compassion is to change how we perceive ourselves. We need to view our work as a way of fulfilling a specific purpose in our lives. It's an invitation to turn a new leaf and to get more real with yourself.

What would you love to contribute to this world?

Before you go out and take on interviews or start that business venture, make these adjustments. Then discipline yourself to carry out the new changes, and before long, new opportunities to serve fellow human beings will present themselves.

Tips To Empower Yourself At Work

• Define what happiness and success feel and look like for you.

No two people (even empaths) share the same definition when it comes to success and happiness. That means you need to redefine what a successful career or job ought to feel and look like. Make sure you know your values and goals and check to see they align with your work.

• Choose career objectives that bring you the highest satisfaction, not others.

Put your needs first and choose to focus on the goals and objectives that bring out the best in you. Goals that make you come alive and feel a sense of fulfillment as you move toward them. As an empowered empath, you have given up the need to do what others expect. You recognize that tending to your needs actually makes you better and creates that energy that's needed to support others without sacrificing yourself.

• Seek a mentor or community that gets you.
Having a guide as you progress in your career whether you choose to be employed or self-employed is vital to your success. That's why every successful individual in the world has at least one mentor. The good news is that you can have a mentor who is also an empath or a highly sensitive person. Someone who is empowered and demonstrates how to live the kind of life you aspire to have. In today's world (thanks to technology) this is easy to arrange. But even if for whatever reason getting a guide isn't possible you can always find a supportive community of like-minded people.

- Don't take things personally.

Most people are usually projecting their unresolved issues and insecurities when they interact with you. Learn to be more light-hearted with other people's comments and opinion.

- Align with your soul and listen to your intuition more before taking action.

Since you play the game of energy, it is crucial to align yourself fully and bring in that higher aspect of you into your daily activities. This will enable you to receive more intuitive guidance and make your actions more productive.

- Set clear energetic boundaries.

Even if you work in an open space in a chaotic office, you can create a sacred "zone" for yourself around your desk with the energetic frequency you want to be in. Using plants, pictures of loved ones or pets or other creative fun ways can create a psychological barrier.

• Create the right atmosphere for yourself.

Do you prefer silence or some background music? Learn to recognize the sights, sounds, smells and other elements that foster a calm, productive state. Find ways to incorporate these things into your workspace whether you work in an office or at home.

• Take frequent breaks to recharge.

It's essential to take short walks, bathroom breaks, water breaks and even short meditative breaks throughout the workday. Many offices today are also creating a uniquely quiet space where one can refuel during the day. If you work from home, then make sure you create a space that enables you to this or schedule short walks around the block.

• Focus on and gravitate toward coworkers that inspire and energize you. Invest your free time on people who uplift you, make you laugh and support your creativity so your time can be more taken up by inspiration. This will help fuel your mood, problem-solving skills, and productivity.

- Choose to make your work about creating meaning and serving others. This is a mindset shift that only you can make. If you decide that your work can and will make a difference in the world, then everything you do will be influenced by that attitude of mind. Don't be reactive; be proactive in all that you do. Your work might be demanding with crazy deadlines but only you can reframe it into something empowering that makes you feel like you're contributing positively.

Chapter 05: Empaths and Self Care

Self-care is crucial to thriving for empaths and highly sensitive people. That includes taking care of yourself both inside and out. In this chapter, we are devoting all our attention to the practices that will help us nurture ourselves first. As all empaths know, putting our needs first is usually quite challenging. As empaths, we naturally extend love outwards and shower others with boundless compassion, affection, and generosity. But have you noticed how hard it can be to point that same level of affection and attention inward?

The very gift that makes us highly attuned to others and their energy combined with our natural tendency to be over giving can spiral into negativity if we neglect our needs. You may not fully believe that you deserve to give yourself the same gifts you often give to others (even those who don't deserve it), but I assure you, no one is more deserving. And you probably need it more than anyone else given all the hardships you've had to endure. Giving is only good to you and the receiver when you give from a place of abundance and overflow. Yet many empaths ignore this natural law of success. In fact, most of us fall into depression, anxiety and we suffer from things like insomnia precisely because we forget to point our gifts inward.

Let's touch on that a bit more here.

Adrenal Fatigue, Exhaustion, and Insomnia. Breaking free of the zombie life.

Adrenal fatigue is a condition many empaths will be familiar with. It is a collection of symptoms such as anxiety, insomnia, body aches, trouble thinking clearly, anxiety and exhaustion. The theory around this condition is that the adrenal glands and hormones such as cortisol that keep you energized start getting depleted because they are unable to deal with the external stress you are exposed to. Given the sensitive nature of empaths, when one hasn't yet developed into an empowered empath, it's easy to see how the daily sensory overload and stressful conditions can quickly lead to such an illness. Unfortunately, toxic people, toxic environments and feeling powerless can lead to endless pain issues and diseases.

Have you ever tossed and turned in bed for hours because you just couldn't fall asleep because of how hyperactive your mind was? Your body might be tired, but if your mind and emotions don't calm down, getting peaceful rest is dreadful. What's worse is that after a while you begin to experience emotional and physical fatigue because you're not recharging. At the beginning of this book, I shared with you the story of how awful things used to be in my world. I would wake up sick and tired, literally. My body ached, I was exhausted and stressed and felt like a needed a reset button. But there was none. My body was under so much stress, and my adrenal glands were terribly over stimulated so I would go from having lots of energy and not being able to sleep for a few weeks then take a dip to the other side where I felt like I had no energy to get up and shower.

At first, I tried to remedy the lack of energy with coffee and sugar, which was a huge mistake. In the end, I had to get some professional help because I finally broke into full-blown insomnia and adrenal fatigue.

It's not easy taking full responsibility for your own emotions and still being able to handle all the energy around you. Especially in our current society. As our minds try to figure out what's happening to combat the discomfort we experience, we must do our part to increase self-awareness so we can recognize what's happening. So in all this discomfort, what should you do?

• Regularly get your cortisol levels measured. Keep a close eye on that and if you're really not in a good place, have your physician prescribe a natural cortisol replacement to help you get back in shape.

• Rest as much as you can. Please sleep for more hours. I cannot emphasize this enough. When I was struggling the most, I was also sleeping the least. There is a direct correlation between how much good sleep you get and how good you feel.

• Learn to manage incoming energy in better more empowering ways. As often as possible "return to sender" the energy that you've picked up which doesn't serve you.

• Create bedtime rituals that take you to a happy place and foster harmony.

• Stay away from stimulants like coffee. If you must have it, don't do it close to your bedtime.

- Work on your mindset and choose to empower yourself so that you can be more in charge and in control of how you feel.

These are just a few things you can already start doing today to help eliminate the struggle that so many of us face. Walking around like a zombie is no fun and messes with your productivity and progress in life.

To counter all the negativity that usually proceeds when an empath neglects his or her own needs, I will be sharing a long list of practices you can start implementing into your daily routine. Pick and choose a handful and test them out to see which resonate with you the most. Not all these practices will suit you so don't feel pressure to use something just because you were told it works. We are all unique and what works for me may not yield highly positive results for another.

If you are a parent raising an empathic or highly sensitive child, these tips are a great way to help them handle their sensitivities better, but you may want to tweak them a bit depending on your particular situation and the age of your child.

One more thing before we start getting into practices. Don't do this from a place of obligation or because your guru says you must. If you're not yet sold on the importance of prioritizing self-care then educate yourself some more on the benefits. Then check in with yourself to see what things feel like currently and compare and contrast the changes that would come about if you were to make the shit.

Importance of Self Care For An Empath And Highly Sensitive People

Self-nurturing, self-compassion, and self-care are integral to the healing of your relationship with yourself. This is what you need if you want to feel whole, fulfilled and secure in this life. Many of us go searching for this feeling in all the wrong places. We seek it in others, in dream jobs, in intimate relationships and so on but the only place we can find it is in the healing of the Self. Learning to love yourself is perhaps one of the biggest jobs you'll ever do because as you start working on yourself, you'll realize there are a lot of self-worth issues to overcome.

By choosing to tend to your own needs and prioritize self-care, you'll start feeling more in charge of your own emotions and sensitivities. You'll no longer feel like you're "too fragile" or at the mercy of other people. There will also be a sense of relief as you go about your day and things will start to feel more balanced. It's definitely going to get easier for you to say no when it feels right for you because in essence your intuition will become strengthened. Exerting healthy boundaries (something many of us struggle with) for yourself and others will feel less awkward, and no one will shame or guilt you into taking time for yourself. I also discovered in my own journey that I had more clarity, an increased mental focus, more energy and I felt more inspired to work on the projects that matter to me. Self-care isn't just about taking care of your physical needs although it does include that. Real self-care includes nourishing your mind, body, and spirit.

Physical self-care is a common one. It involves taking care of your body internally and externally. This includes eating the right food, self-grooming, engaging in some form of physical activity regularly, getting enough sleep and staying hydrated.

Mental self-care is just as important as physical self-care and involved giving your mind just the right amount of stimulation to keep it sharp, active and focused. This can be done through reading, engaging in deep conversation with someone you strongly connect with or even listening to inspiring podcasts and learning something new.

Emotional self-care gives us the mastery we need to step out of survival mode and into thriving mode as empaths. Because we detect and process energy at heightened levels, emotional self-care is something we cannot afford to skip over. Our emotional well-being and overall health depend on it because what we hold on the inside materializes on the outside as our reality. That's why we must engage daily in some form of emotional processing and release of feelings that are active within us. We can do it with a trusted friend, journal it down, or speak to a therapist. We can also choose fun ways to help us dissolve and release negative emotions through composing music, listening to music, dancing, drawing, poetry singing, etc.

Spiritual self-care is something no one can ever tell you how to do it right. It is such a personal and intimate experience that only you can discover through your own sacred experiments. Spiritual self-care means different things to different people and usually comes down to the ideologies you hold. Maybe you associate it with cultural tradition, or perhaps for you, it's religious. Regardless of your concept, what matters is that you are nurturing yourself spiritually. It's one of the most important aspects of self-care especially if you are looking to eradicate that feeling of loneliness, "not belonging," feeling unloved and alone. A permanent and real sense of oneness, belonging, connectedness and self-acceptance take place when you feed yourself spiritually either through reading spiritual books, Yoga, Meditation, spending time in nature and other spiritual practices. In the last chapter, we dive more into spiritual awakening and what that means for an empath so if you've been curious about this topic keep turning the pages.

Life-supporting activities also require some conscious self-care because these are the practical things that make your life more comfortable. Things like housework chores, grocery shopping, finances, and logistics are all tasks that can at times feel burdensome, and that drains our energy. However, we can choose to practice a little self-care and self-awareness as we go through these tasks, which helps us feel a sense of accomplishment. For example, I decided I would rearrange the furniture in my home using Feng Shui. I decluttered my closet and set up a little "calm zone" area for myself. I am also getting into the habit of setting up auto-pay on my essential monthly bills so that I don't have to deal with running late on my payments. And I consciously watch my inner dialogue whenever I am paying for things in the supermarket or at a restaurant because I want my money talk to shift from lack to abundance. These little shifts that I am prioritizing are taking mundane everyday chores and turning them into moments where I can deliberately practice self-love.

All this to say that self-care is something that must capture all aspects of your life. Leave no area unattended especially the daily mundane stuff that usually burdens you. Use every opportunity to show yourself how much you care and love yourself. The more you can give to yourself and evoke within you that feeling of being loved and cared for, the easier it will be to give to others from a place of overflow. The trick here is to hold the right energy space for others as you manage and master your own emotions and energy.

Finding Your True Self

Before you can really embrace, accept and love yourself fully you must shift the perception you hold about who you really are. What does it really mean to you to be your true Self?

Do you currently feel like you are being yourself? And do you even like yourself? For many empaths, saying yes requires effort. Too many false conditioning and low self-esteem stand in the way of that positive perception. But here's the thing... To thrive as an empath, you must be yourself. And to be yourself, you've got to know who you are. Your sense of identity and the self-image you hold about yourself will never allow you to step into a state of empowerment unless you build a strong, stable ground from which to stand. For a long time, I used to say, " I just want to be myself but I don't know how." It was the imprisoned aspect of me that was seeking freedom. But freedom from what?

This is a profound question that requires contemplation, reflection, and lifelong exploration because we are all seeking that same freedom. What I'm sure of is that this freedom can only happen when we begin to realize there is a version of us "invisible to the outside world" that holds all the answers. And part of practicing self-care is acknowledging that the more we point self-compassion, forgiveness, self-love, and affection inward, the more we are inviting this other "Self" to flow into our consciousness and actively engage with us. There is great power in this and as any empowered empath will tell you, learning to open up to and connect with that other Self will give your whole life new meaning and shed light on why you are here and why you possess the gifts and sensitivities that make you an empath.

I hope you are starting to see why self-care isn't just something nice to do for yourself; it is the key to the freedom that you seek.

Locating And Healing Your Emotional Triggers

We all have those super-reactive buttons inside of us that become activated by someone else's behavior, comment or energy. It is imperative we become aware of these buttons so we can create a buffer time to help us avoid that natural tendency to become reactive. Our human mind is inherently impatient and has all kinds of hang-ups and emotional reactions especially when our ideas about how things should be collide with how things are. As empaths, we are experts at self-torment and self-manufactured pain whether we realize it or not. Usually, it's because we make choices, say things or hold ourselves back and postpone our happiness because we don't feel deserving enough. It seems we've become so accustomed to "settling" for coping mechanisms and survival guides that no other life seems possible at present. When something is always missing or when we still feel inferior to the present circumstances, it becomes easy to fall for the trap of self-loathing and judgment. This can be a great source of emotional pain. A wound is created, and whenever someone happens to press on that wound, we immediately react. Through the mind, many of us have created a prison of suffering (empaths all believe in the great suffering), and we forget that we are the architects of our lives. You hold the key that can and will set you free.

Read that last statement several times. Breathe it in, contemplate, pray and meditate over it until it feels true for you because in reality, until you start believing that you hold the key to freedom and success, the "great suffering" will continue to consume you. By becoming aware of and uncovering the false perceptions that cause you to cling to pain and suffering you can open up to a deep experience of peace and heal your triggers. For example, if someone tells you that you don't have what it takes to manifest true love in your life because you can only attract narcissists, and you overreact, it indicates there's a trigger there. There must be a place in you that is emotionally wounded by that statement. Is it because that has been your past experience? Is it because that's what you secretly believe as well? Or could it be that you don't feel worthy of love?

When you catch yourself reacting, lashing out, getting defensive, angry or resentful, stop, breathe, distance yourself from that heated moment and address your emotional issues. You might think that the other person is wrong for being so rude and insensitive, but in actuality, if you hadn't allowed other forces and factors to dictate your behavior, you'd have no reason to be affected by this. Being aware of your actions and behavior rather than dwelling on what the other person is doing or saying is where you need to focus your attention. Your emotional triggers are wounds that need to heal. The best way to do this is by practicing self-compassion and mental cleansing. You need to know what beliefs you hold and why you still hold them. Many empaths have grown up in environments that traumatized them emotionally, and so it's only natural that some of those wounds still need healing. For example, children who grew up feeling helpless will probably experience panic and overwhelm whenever they're in a new situation. And if assigned large projects with very little time they might crack under that pressure, not because they're not good enough but because the workload triggers a wound that still needs healing. If someone around makes a comment around their inability to perform the task properly, this triggers an emotional and sometimes physical reaction that can lead to anger, binge eating, over drinking, etc. The best way to free yourself from such experiences now and in the future is by learning to release and heal those wounds. When you find yourself overcome by negative emotions, test out some of these tips to see which ones bring you back to peace and well-being.

Tip One: Resist the natural impulse to judge your feelings as bad and definitely don't ignore them. Every emotion you experience believe it or not can teach you something about yourself. Ask what the emotion is trying to tell you and listen with great intent as your body picks up the message.

Tip Two: Practice self-compassion as soon as you catch yourself falling for the negative energies. Speak words of encouragement and love. You can say, "this too shall pass" or "whatever fear says, I know nothing can destroy me." Cling to the knowing that regardless of what's happening, the real you is strong and bigger than any condition.

Tip Three: Switch your perspective and be more objective about your emotions. As you catch yourself being sucked into a negative spiral, rather than resist (what you resist persists) simply ground yourself and let that energy flow. If you identify with negativity and acknowledge "I am angry" or "I am depressed," it's super hard to detach and let go. That's why you want to train yourself to see emotions as moving energy like electricity. Think of a beautiful chandelier hanging in a hotel lobby. When the lights are switched on, electricity flows and illuminates the chandelier. We can distinguish that moving electricity is not the chandelier. Similarly, your emotions flow through you, but they are not who you really are.

Tip Four: Perhaps this is the first tip I should have started with because it truly is the starting point of any transformation. Take full responsibility over your life and the emotions that dominate your day. If you catch yourself reacting to certain people and situations in the same way, rather than label them bad, ask yourself what you need to learn and do to change that automatic response.

Tip Five: Be willing to heal your emotions. Don't let your ego tell you that there's something wrong with you or worse yet, that there's nothing you can do about how others make you feel. The reactions you experience are only responses and even though you might not always know what to do to heal, simply declaring that you are open, willing and ready to heal allows the process to begin.

Tip Six: Journal about the origin of your triggers as you become aware of them. If like in the example I shared above you realize something happened while you were a child that caused you to feel wounded, now you have the opportunity to rewrite that story with greater awareness. Once you track and find the origin of the emotional wound, I want you to tear off those pages of the old story, burn or shred them into pieces then start again with the new permanent story that you want to attach to that phase of your past.

Tip Seven: Reprogram your false beliefs as you become aware of the triggers. Start with the trigger that has the least emotional charge. Compassionately tell yourself "this is not my reality anymore. What is true is that I am deserving of love, I am intelligent, I am capable of greatness, I am good enough." Whatever wound you still have, find it's ideal opposite and replace the old conviction with this new one.

Tip Eight: If this feels too much for you to bear, consider getting assistance from a trained professional or at the very least, a trusted loved one. Surround yourself with people you love and respect, let them know what you're working on so they can help you during those reactive moments. If you don't want to do this with a family member or friend you could choose to join a group therapy or seek expert help from someone trained in the field of psychiatry or emotional trauma. Just make sure it is someone you naturally vibe with because having that natural chemistry will aid the healing you want to experience.

Nutrition And Exercise

Before you can find peace, freedom, and a sense of fulfillment and thrive in your life, you must find harmony. Moreso, what I am referring to here is inner harmony and what's commonly referred to as homeostasis.

This is a quest many human beings are on whether consciously or unconsciously because whenever the physical body is not in homeostasis, nothing else really works. Do you agree?

Well, for empaths and highly sensitive people the urgency of creating good eating habits is more pronounced. The way I like to say it is that we have a short karmic leash. We can't get away with half of what the average human can do whether that means indulging with negativity, binge-eating or neglecting our bodies. If we don't cleanse our energy and generate productive emotions, we suffer more than the average person. Similarly, if we don't eat right, we'll feel the negative consequences of that decision more intensely. Our ability to function productively will be significantly hindered which in turn will negatively impact all other areas of our lives such as relationships and work. It, therefore, goes without saying that to become the healthiest version of yourself, you'll have to understand and take better care of your body and mind. The more harmonious your mind-body connection is, the happier, energetic, productive and resilient you will be.

There's a wonderful conversation that Dr. Deepak Chopra and Oprah Winfrey had back in the '90s (when women had really strange hairstyles). And in my opinion, I think the lessons shared on that day can greatly benefit us as empaths today. Dr. Chopra taught that every person has a body type and that knowing one's body type is the easiest way to find inner balance and harmony. He went on to share the three body types and how we can know which one applies to each of us, but he also mentioned that some of us might actually be a combination of more than one. And that is okay too. Gaining an awareness of which one or two body types you are is what matters because with this knowledge you'll make better choices with your eating, exercising and resting habits.

Another critical thing that I took away from watching that conversation is something Dr. Chopra said. He said, "Whenever you react to anything whether it's a traffic jam, criticism from your boss, a love note, rainy weather, or a headache, you're really reacting not to the external signal, but to something that you generate within yourself. And if you become aware of that and you become aware of your tendencies, then you can change things in your life. Whether that's food, relationships, environment or the way you manage stress and bring about balance. So knowing your body type helps you to create more balance in your body."

That is such powerful stuff. You should probably read it repeatedly. If you have chosen to become an empowered empath, this type of insight is invaluable because it helps guide your actions and the changes that you can start making within and without. Instead of treating nutrition and exercise as an obligation, they become intentional choices you make because you have a deeper understanding of your body and the connection it has with your sense of inner harmony and well-being. Naturally, your inner harmony and well-being will become projected into outer reality. Therefore I see this topic of taking care of your diet and making sure you regularly move your body as something enjoyable. It is a lifestyle choice that continues to aid you as you grow and thrive in society.

Healthy eating habits:
This is about nourishing your body with foods and beverages that are good for your body. Foods that help you soothe your sensitivities. For empaths and highly sensitive people, we know that stimulants aren't very good for us so it would be wise to reduce or eliminate anything that over stimulates your body and sensory system. Fresh fruits and vegetables have high water content and are very rich in fiber so these should be a priority for us. They also contain antioxidants, which help keep the skin looking younger.

Omega 3 fatty acids reduce stress, and we all know how hyperactive our bodies are so it would be a good idea to include Omega 3 into your diet. I am a great fan of black tea and Vitamin C as I find it helps to reduce my stress hormones and protect my immune system, but I would recommend reducing the intake of high carbonated foods as much as possible. This isn't a book on diet, and you can find plenty of books that dive into specific diets you can try out. My intention here is to drive a simple point home: With our sensitivities, hyperactive nervous systems and all the energy we process daily, a balanced diet that works for our body type is imperative. It will prevent unhealthy food cravings, fuel us and enable us to fight off anything detrimental to our bodies.

Regularly moving your body:
Like it or not, exercise is good for your physical, mental and emotional well-being. In fact, when I skip my regular workout for an extended period, my emotions become a bit overwhelming. Exercising helps me enhance my sense of well-being, happiness, emotional balance, and my relationships. It can also be a great stress buster or a fast way of breaking

negative stagnant energy that's threatening your inner peace.

Science has now proven that even a little bit of regular exercising can help you fight depression, anxiety, loneliness and it boosts self-confidence. In other words, all the negative stuff that usually keep a disempowered empath feeling stuck and miserable can be overcome by integrating regular workouts into your routine.

Now, I know what you might be thinking... "I hate going to the gym" or "I don't have an hour every day for the gym!"

This isn't about going to the gym, and it doesn't matter how much time you have. You can exercise anywhere you want. At home, at the park, in your hotel room and so on. You are limited by your level of creativity. And if you have an excellent workout routine, even twenty minutes is enough to get you going. Consider cycling, power walks, Zumba classes, Salsa lessons, martial arts, Yoga, Pilates, Cross Fit, jogging just to name a few. If traditional workouts don't work for you, find something that does. Again, going back to what Dr. Chopra said, it's about understanding yourself and what you need to find inner balance.

A great place to start knowing more about your body and what it needs is to learn more about the Ayurvedic body types, (also known as Doshas) and seeing which type feels more like you. Let me briefly share what the three body types are and how they react under stress. Then I encourage you to go research more about your Aryuvedic body type so you can see the best way to nourish and exerc

What is your Dosha or Body Type?

Vata: If you're a Vata body type then you're light, flexible and tend not to gain weight or muscle easily. You are hyper metabolic meaning you can basically eat anything you want and never gain weight. Usually very enthusiastic and full of energy but when under stress or pressure you'll quickly fall into anxiety, suffer from insomnia, have muscle spasm, migraine headaches, etc.

Pitta: If you're a Pitta then you have a muscular, athletic build. You are brave, courageous and articulate. You're like a fiery metabolic and when under stress you can get impatient, and suffer from ulcer, hypertension and heart attacks, etc.

Kapha: If you're a Kapha then you're friendly, joyful, vivacious and compassionate. You'd be considered hypo metabolic and typically tend to have extra body fat. When under stress you tend to hold on to things whether that's food, relationships, etc.

Again, this is just a brief description of each of the three doshas and by digging a little deeper using the research links provided at the end of this book. You can also do some of the simple dosha tests offered by platforms like the Chopra Center.

- Food dilemmas for empaths and highly sensitive people.

Figuring out the right diet plan or what to eat on a day-to-day basis can be quite a challenge for us, which might become overwhelming, and we don't want that. We know that if we eat too little, we'll get light headed, feel exhausted, anxious, jittery and probably crave things that aren't good for our bodies. We also know overeating is a terrible experience, so I recommend you research on the types of diets that feel interesting to you now that you understand a little more about your body type. Test out a few and modify them to fit your lifestyle. As a general rule of thumb, here's what I think works across the board.

• Build your diet around high fiber foods like fruits and vegetables. If you have things like protein, nuts, seeds, and whole grain make sure they are high quality and "sit well" with your digestion.

• Eat bigger portions at the start of the day and lower the sizes, as the day gets older. By reducing the quantity (not the quality) of your food intake as the day comes to an end, you give your body ample time to digest, and you can also use that fuel during the day when you need it most. I also find eating lighter in the evenings helps me sleep comfortably.

• Stay super hydrated throughout the day. The more hydrated you are, the sharper your brain will be, and it will help you escape the trap of snacking on junk food every hour. A great way to avoid the support of caffeinated drinks is to have more water as fatigue is directly related to dehydration. The more active you are (if working out etc.), the more water you'll need to drink that day.

• Try to avoid going on extreme crash diets or extreme detox regimes. It's okay to do a light detox from time to time, but strict juice fasts are not something I recommend. This is because such extreme fluid fasts strain the body's digestive system and organs and are quite exhausting. As an empath, this self-induced stress can be misinterpreted poorly causing the body to go into fight or flight mode instead of "detox and rest" mode.

After everything we've shared so far, I hope it is becoming clear that increasing your level of awareness is key. Becoming more aware of your body type, how your body reacts to specific foods and the types of diets and exercises that bring out the healthiest version of you is the best way to enjoy the healthy lifestyle you want. It all comes down to your willingness to self-educate and self-study so you can make better, stronger choices.

Now, let's talk about practical ways you can practice self-care daily.

Tips For Self-Care

• Practice self-forgiveness daily.

Create a customized ritual that you go through each day to self-reflect and take responsibility for your actions and energy. Taking some time each day to observe yourself as an outsider and notice how you reacted or behaved in certain situations enables you to learn and grow from your mistakes rather than unconsciously punishing yourself. This is what self-compassion is all about. Take your mistakes, mishaps, disappointments or any other scenarios where you didn't show up as your best self and reframe those mistakes as lessons. See them as your opportunity for self-discovery and growth.

- Get more sleep

Everyone needs to get adequate sleep. This is a topic that has been getting a lot of attention even in the business world with successful individuals like Arianna Huffington advocating the importance of sleeping more in a sleep-deprived society. For empaths and highly sensitive people, sleeping more is just as important as eating right and exercising. Our nervous system is hyperactive and continually working on processing all the bits and data around us. When we sleep, we have the chance to de-stress and reset the nervous system. We give it a break from all the sensory overload, giving us more power to function better the next day. Everyone is different, so you need to figure out your optimum sleep time. Most people require a minimum of 8 hours every night. Start with going to bed an hour earlier this week and take note of the change in focus, emotional stability and how rested you feel.

- Exercise.

Not everyone enjoys going to the gym, but exercising isn't about hitting the gym. It's about moving your body and breaking a sweat while enjoying it. If going to the gym doesn't excite you find something that will. Try doing Yoga, Pilates, cycling, jogging in the park, martial arts, and hula hooping or dancing. Mix things up, combine a few routines to make your own and create a routine that you can sustain as a lifestyle.

- Check in with your body at regular intervals throughout the day. This is called practicing mindfulness. Stop at intervals, breathe and acknowledge yourself. Notice how you feel in body, mind, and spirit. If you sense negativity or any kind of discomfort deal with it immediately. Don't allow things to snowball as it becomes tough to handle yourself when you stop being in charge of your inner state.

- Meditate.

This is one of the easiest ways to instantly practice self-care, ground yourself and reconnect your mind-body-spirit. Some people (including me) cannot survive a day without mediating. Others don't find it so useful. It's necessary to give it a try before assuming it won't work for you. Encourage yourself and practice some patience if you're just learning how to meditate because, for the most part, I know those who turn it into a ritual find it hard to ever go back. Meditation is so powerful because it reduces stress and creates a stronger connection with the whole of your being. It can also be a great way to go within and gain some clarity and insight when you need guidance about your life.

- Distance yourself from toxic people and toxic situations.

It's time to choose your inner circle more cautiously. Now that you understand how porous you are to your environment surround yourself with people who will uplift, encourage, inspire and support you. Gravitate toward positive people with generous, loving energy and cut down the time you spend with relatives or colleagues who don't bring out the best in you. The stronger and more empowered you become as you continue to develop yourself, the easier it will be to distance yourself physically and emotionally from those that aren't for your highest good. This will take practice and some courage especially when you realize some of the toxic people are blood relatives, but each time you step away from those dark energy spots, you'll be performing an act of self-care and self-love.

• Take time to process your emotions.
Identify and locate the emotion physically as soon as you become aware of it. Then set aside a few minutes, calm yourself and allow yourself to process what you're feeling. Make sure you choose to do this where you won't be disturbed. With your eyes closed, connect with

your body and that energy; observe it first as yourself, then as an undetached detective. Witness this experience without judgment and let your attention pass through your body as you observe the sensations that are coming up. Now, express the feeling and place your hand on the part of your body where you feel that energy the strongest. For example, if it's a tight chest, place your hand on your chest and say it out loud, "it hurts here."

If you can't say it out loud, then consider writing it out on a piece of paper. Be aware that whatever you are feeling is happening inside your body and that you are fully responsible. This isn't about making yourself feel guilty, ashamed, weak or wrong. You always have the power to interpret the experience in any way you choose. Recognize that you always have the ability to respond to any adverse situation in a new and creative way. No one has power over you; not even your sensitivities. Hold this understanding in your consciousness for a few minutes as you release that energy. Continue placing your hand on that part of your body that feels discomfort and with every exhalation of your breath, have the intention of releasing that tension. Do this for the next 30 seconds. Feel the sensation leaving your body with every breath.

• Connect with nature.

American author Elizabeth Gilbert wrote a short piece entitled " Go to the Water" that I think nails this idea home for us. I know you already know the deep connection experienced when you're out in nature, but I want to encourage it even more.

Dear Ones - Years ago when I was going through a really hard time, a friend of mine who was a naturalist gave me some beautiful advice about how to best take care of myself. He told me, "when an animal in the wild has been injured, it has only two strategies for how to heal itself: It can rest, or it can go to the water. Right now, try to do as much of both as possible."

Make it a daily habit to connect with nature as much as you can. Soak in some sun, hug a tree, or if you're fortunate enough to live in a location where you can go to the water.

• Practice gratitude daily.

This is one of the most powerful rituals you can integrate into your life.

Zig Ziglar said, "Gratitude is the healthiest of all human emotions. The more you express gratitude for what you have, the more likely you will have even more to express gratitude for." I couldn't have said it better myself. If you want to become a thriving empath, this is the secret sauce that gets you there. Gratitude will shift your mood and energy instantly. Regardless of what's going on in your life or who is around you, if you can come back into the state of gratitude and focus on what you can appreciate, feel deep thankfulness for and praise then you will immediately feel the shift.

- Journal.

Get into the daily habit of being with your thoughts for a few minutes. It can be to self reflect on the day, to make intentions at the beginning of the day, to give gratitude for the things that really matter to you or a combination at different intervals. Journaling can also be a great way to help you process emotions because you can acknowledge how your feeling, name it, tame it and release it.

- Practice being in the present moment.

Most of the time we get overwhelmed or anxious because we allow our thoughts to move to a future or past event which we honestly can't control. The only time that is in your control is the time you presently have. Be more in the now and choose to do the best you can with what you've got right where you are. You'll be surprised how much power this gives you, especially when presented with a situation that threatens your peace of mind.

- Chunk down your workload and goals.

Since we know how quickly we can get overwhelmed, it becomes necessary to organize our workload and schedules in a way that promotes harmony. Planning things in advance and chunking things down further into tasks that feel small enough is actually an act of self-care. It helps you reduce procrastination and gives you the feeling of confidence needed to accomplish what you set out to do.

- Take a soothing bath.

I find this works very well for many empaths and highly sensitive people. You can take baths daily or a few times a week with your favorite salt bath and essential oils. I also like to add some scented candles and my favorite soothing music in the background just to give myself that extra treat. 30 minutes later I usually come out of that experience feeling reborn.

- Listen to music.

Music is my first love. It's my first go-to place when I need to practice self-care and self-love. I find that music has a potent effect on my mood and can aid in lowering pain, stress levels, and even my heart rate. Obviously, the type of music one listens to matters a lot; so it goes without saying, choose your music wisely. Let it be music that soothes you and brings you back to your happy place.

Chapter 06: Spirituality And Transcending Limitations As An Empath

This last chapter is devoted to those of us who are realizing that there's more to being an empath than just having a hyperactive nervous system. If you've already been studying the path of being an empath and something in you still feels like "there's more to it than what the books say," I encourage you to pay extra attention to this section. Aletheia Luna said, "One of the greatest advantages of being an empath is that experiencing a spiritual awakening is virtually inevitable. In other words, spiritually awakening seems to be written into our DNA."

We are going to shed some light on the link between being an empath and spiritual awakening. A lot of people think spirituality is wishy-washy stuff and not practical enough to be understood, but that isn't accurate. I intend to bring greater clarity into your awareness so that if you are on a path of spiritual awakening, you can quickly rise to the higher states that are even now summoning you. How will you know if there is a higher calling at play in your life? Let's start with a few signs to look out for.

• An increased and keen awareness (deep sadness and compassion) about the suffering in the world. It isn't just about your personal suffering, it's that you feel a connection with the deep despair and depression that people are experiencing in today's society.

• An increased sensation of love will also burst into your experience. You feel deep compassion for the suffering in the world, but you also feel an overwhelming love that you just want to pour into everything and everyone. You can see more clearly the world in all of its beauty not just in nature but in the people as well.

- You can feel something inside you has shifted. You're no longer the same person even though you can't fully articulate it. There's an undeniable sensation that you have become a new person; you're different, and the world seems different to you.

- Negative habits are more, and you can quickly tell what's not right in your "old life" and what must change now that you feel like a new person. Certain things that you used to tolerate or do are now intolerable. It just feels like you're ready for a change and you can't go back.

- You are experiencing insanely vivid dreams that don't make complete sense, but that give you a sense of peace. It could be that the dreams are helping pass on the insights and inner truth you've been seeking all your life.

- Synchronistic experiences happen more and more often. This means you're experiencing meaningfully related events that are too good to be a coincidence. For example, the thought of a friend you haven't seen for years crosses your mind and later that day they give you a call. You think about an old favorite song from a decade ago, and when you turn on the radio, it's the first song that plays.

These experiences tend to guide us toward a path, but sometimes, they show us to remind us that we are already on the right path.

Finding Peace And Freedom

Every human being on the planet wants to have more peace and freedom in their lives. It has increasingly become important in society as the global consciousness begins the shift from chasing after career success, money and other surface-level goals to more eternal desires. For empaths and highly sensitive people, the quest runs deeper because we already feel chained and suppressed in society. Trying to fit in, creating coping mechanisms to help us lead lives that are socially appropriate even if it's not what we desire causes us to crave freedom even more. Nothing is more elusive than peace, especially inner peace. It can feel as though forces outside your control are in charge, but this isn't fundamentally true. To step into an experience where peace and a sense of freedom is your daily reality, you must first learn to create peace within and then all around you. The world's wisdom traditions all teach that the source of violence, war, rebellion, and unrest lies inside each of us. That includes you!

The fact that you can tune in to so many emotions and energies around you and allow them to dominate your day implies that you are using your sensitivities and gifts to perpetuate more of this dark energy. Of course, this is not to imply that it's your fault. If you haven't learned how to use your powers positively, then it's unlikely you'd be able to transcend negative energies. But when you develop yourself and become an amplifier of peace consciousness then in a very significant way, you contribute to world peace. Before you can exemplify this quality, you must first develop and embody it. The journey begins with you creating inner peace. Inner reality creates outer reality.

Dr. Deepak Chopra, an expert on this topic, tells us that finding peace and freedom begins with seeking and finding the peace that lies within. Meditation and Yoga are the tools he recommends we leverage because each of these tools enables us to look inside ourselves and create that body-mind-spirit connection.

For Dr. Chopra, this search involves transcending superficial mental activity and ordinary thinking to reach the deepest parts of our minds where peace resides. There is a place within you that is a sacred refuge; a place where you feel genuinely at peace and whole. Finding this place is a journey of a thousand miles that requires no physical effort whatsoever. Anyone can begin this journey at any point of their lives, and although it is challenging, it is well worth the mental, emotional and spiritual effort.

Here are the 4 tips Dr. Chopra shares how to do it. You'll find a link to this resource at the end of the book as well if you want to look it up and dive deeper.

Tip 1. Locate your zone of peace. This is done by going inward and transcending the constant activity of the mind.

Tip 2. Regularly return to this place of peace and make it your home. Let it be your grounding center. Whenever conditions destabilize or stress you or negative emotions come flooding in, find your way back to the zone of peace immediately. This is going to be challenging at first, but with practice, it will get easier.

Tip 3. Let go of all aspects of violence. What? I'm not into violence, I hate it! I hear you say. But the truth is, without meaning to, empaths are unconsciously participating in acts of violence. How? Resentment, entertaining negative energy, envy, anger and so on. Wasting your energy pointing fingers, feeling angry and hurt by your past, talking about energy vampires in your life and hating them for making you feel so bad is not an act of peace. Think about it for a moment.

You can never fight against anything and create something positive. An angry peacemaker ceases to be a peacemaker because no peace can be found in non-peace. It's therefore vital for us as empaths to be vigilant of our egos, judgment of ourselves and others, our insecurities and the negative emotions that are active within. Dr. Chopra encourages you us to meditate until we become accustomed to the peaceful self within us who is not the ego self we know.

Tip 4. Become more intentional and allowing of your peaceful self to show up in everyday experiences. This is going to be a challenge because you encounter all types of energies and emotions. However, Dr. Chopra says that you have the power to choose to follow the silent voice of the true self and amplify that powerful peace-filled energy so much so that it drowns out the loud negative energies all around you. This requires you to stop being passive and dormant with your energy. It also requires you to release your own resentments, anger, and other emotional baggage so that the energy of love, calmness, and creativity can take over.

Be in the flow of life and let go of your imposed limitations because as long as you argue for those lower energies, you won't have access to the realm that holds the peace and freedom you yearn for. The good news is, the zone of peace is real and empowered empaths know how to prioritize it above all other experiences. Will you choose to do the same?

Spiritual awakening: The five stages

When going through a spiritual awakening, we experience emotions and energy way more than usual and at times that can be quite painful. It's like turning up the volume to full blast on your iPod while wearing your earphones. The song might be great, but your ears won't enjoy it.

As such, it's super tough to function and comfortably manage daily duties because everything is so intense and exaggerated. Add to that the natural ability to also pick up on other people's "stuff" and it's likely your awakening will feel more like a breakdown than a breakthrough.

There have been times in my life where I could have sworn things were going to hell. Nothing seemed to be moving in the direction of freedom and success that I was aiming for. My emotional and physical well-being seemed to be getting worse, not better. I was overcome with, and it made no sense whatsoever why my body felt so weak. As I connect the dots now, I can recognize (knowing what I know) that there was nothing wrong with me at all. I made it more difficult for myself by resisting it and interpreting the process poorly, so I hope by reading this, you'll avoid making that same mistake. If you're going through the motions of spiritual awakening and you're at that chaotic phase where it seems damn near impossible to maintain your sanity, rest assured that in a little while the storm will pass and you'll awaken to clear blue skies and a perfectly calm sea.

The path to freedom, wholeness, and self-healing is the path of allowing yourself to feel more. I know intense emotions usually cause us to take flight or avoid those uncomfortable feelings, but I encourage you to embrace this experience. The heightened level of sensitivities that you'll feel is what's needed to bring you back into wholeness and healing. While it can be painful, it doesn't need to be, and below I will share some of the things you can do to make this awakening process much more manageable. Before getting to that, I want to share with you a lesson that I found very useful when I started digging into this topic. Mindbodygreen.com teaches that there are 5 stages of spiritual awakening an individual goes through in their life. After going through these five teachings, I realized nothing was wrong in my life, I was simply moving from one level to the next. It helped calm my mind and trust more in the process of life. I want to share with you these five stages from the perspective of an empath and what each step will probably feel like for you.

The Change:
This is the first stage. It's when you fully realize that you really are above ordinary human awareness and that you can see, feel and experience things that others cannot. Growing up, very few of us knew that we are empaths. We ended up believing that there was

something wrong with us, that we are weak and weird.

Well, the moment you awaken to the fact that you have a gift and that your sensitivities serve a purpose on this planet, you enter stage one. Awareness takes place in this first phase. You become keenly aware that you're not just crazy or making stuff up and depending on your state of mind and environment, you could feel a sense of empowerment, or you could feel totally at the mercy of other people. The energies around you increase in intensity, and you become more attuned to your gifts but probably not in a good way. For most of us, the realization that we are different makes us feel worse because we don't feel empowered enough to use this difference positively. Although it is life itself calling us to serve a higher purpose, we often get stuck in a victim mindset, and some even go around teaching it is a curse to be as we are.

The Shift:

Those of us who go through life struggling with the fact that we are aware of the differences and powers that we possess continue to observe and self-reflect. Then we get curious enough to ask a different question.

What if this is a good thing?

As soon as we start thinking along these new lines, we move into the second phase where we become conscious of this inner need to do more and be more. We start wondering if at all it is possible to make a difference in the world and contribute to the community. We seek the chance to be more proactive instead of continually being reactive. It's really hard at first, but the yearning is there to become a better person. Suffering is still part of our reality at this point, but even in the midst of it all, we sense something more is calling us.

The Search:

By the time you and I hit this stage our soul is fully connected with our intellect, and we start craving soul satisfaction. At that point, we are on fire. Like a burning bush that won't die no matter how great the storm is. That's when you would start searching for classes, videos, podcasts, books such as this one or anything else that can give you answers and guidance on how to take the next step forward.

I assume by reading this far, you're more likely in this stage of your awakening. Keep going no matter how difficult the path is because you are well on your way to unfolding the highest version of yourself. Freedom and the peace you've been yearning for all your life is within reach. The more forward momentum you create, the more you will evolve your soul and gain spiritual wisdom.

The Desire:

This is the stage where the real desires of your heart emerge and for the first time (especially after reading this book) you pay close attention to them. You listen to and attend to your needs without feeling guilty or selfish. It also becomes necessary for you to seek our new company so you might notice that you feel like surrounding yourself with like-minded souls and people who are on the same path of spiritual awakening. This is the stage where the stormy seas begin to calm down, and the real cleansing takes place. It feels natural to release any toxins, people who no longer feel right, and habits that aren't for your highest good. The best part is you'll do it with effortless ease.

The Opening:

This is the last stage after much of the cleansing and healing has taken place. It's the empowered state that every empath dreams of experiencing. At this phase of your life, freedom and peace of mind is a daily reality. You're no longer just trying to survive; you're actually thriving as an empath.

The reason this stage is called the opening is that you are more open, welcoming and in control of your power. You've learned to love and accept yourself just as you are. Instead of feeling like a victim in this world because of your powers, you feel empowered by your sensitivities almost like a superhuman because you can do, feel, experience and influence things in a way that most people can't. At this stage in your life, it becomes clear that every change, shift, and desire along this path has led you deeper into the discovery of your own soul and potential. As you finally begin to understand the greater meaning behind your life and sensitivities, you're more open to developing those gifts so that you can become a light that positively impacts this planet. Every little thing that crosses your path, all the people (yes, even the toxic people) become part of a chain to your greater good. You see the lesson that each person helped you learn and how much stronger you've grown as a result of your childhood and past experience. The story is rewritten, and you truly connect to your soul's purpose.

This is my hope for all empaths because I know how much the world needs more highly sensitive and empathic people to rise into power and shift the universal consciousness. Only through the spiritual awakening is this possible because we must first grow, develop and transcend before we can be able to illuminate the path for others. The suffering that's going on in this world won't be eradicated through force, resistance or constriction but through love and compassion.

I can't think of anyone better to start pouring this love and compassion into the world than an empowered empath, can you?

Daily spiritual practices to help you thrive

• Set daily intentions that help you develop and tap into your highest divine potential.

Choose to start each day intentionally. Always think about who you want to be that day and how you want to show up in your work, relationships and with your goals.

• Bring more awareness to the activities you engage in.

In every moment you have the power to bring in more awareness, and it is one of the best daily practices to integrate into your life should you wish to be more spiritually awakened. Ask yourself throughout the day " What am I doing now?" It's such a simple question yet so profound when it comes to bringing our full awareness into the present moment. It's a great way to take yourself out of autopilot reactions.

• Find calming scents that elevate your mood. Many empaths enjoy finding scents and using them in their surrounding daily. Some even include incense burning as part of their daily meditation routine because incense purifies the air and elevates the mood. I have a friend who carries around a small bottle with a special perfume that she takes out several times a day and rubs a few drops on her hands whenever she needs energy soothe. You can also choose to use essentials oils or scented candles depending on where you want to use them.

• Carry spiritual items such as crystal tones, necklace, etc. It can also be an inspirational note in your purse or wallet or a gratitude stone. Some people will hang a set of mala beads on the rearview mirror of the car. I like to keep my earphones close to me because I have spiritually uplifting material on my phone in the form of audio books and music. The purpose of this is to have something you can quickly fall back on the moment you feel you need some spiritual nourishment.

- Meditation. This is by far the most common practice (that even I swear by) if you want to connect with the spiritual aspect of yourself. I don't think it needs to be complicated, just start with 1-minute meditation focusing on your breathing, and as you get better at that, you can employ more advanced measures. There are also lots of apps like Head Space and Chopra Meditation Experience that can guide you through the mastery of this practice. The most important thing is to find a technique that you enjoy.
- Watch your inner dialogue. By choosing to notice the tone and nature of your internal conversation as well as the mind movies you're continually playing throughout the day, it becomes easy to change the things that don't serve you. If like most of us you realize you are your own worst enemy, you'll feel more determined to start changing how you handle yourself. And you can more intentionally welcome higher knowledge and spiritual guidance because spiritual awakening cannot

happen to a mind that is waging war against itself. Remember that the next time you self-loath or self-judge.

• Invest in self-education and spiritual study. Choose to invest in educating and nourishing yourself spiritually. The same way you invest in nourishing, clothing and taking care of your physical body, you must also be interested in advancing your spiritual self. Be curious about your growth as a spiritual being. Do a self-audit every few months to see how your inner world is feeling. Find spiritual teachers, guides and material that support your growth. Choose to build that connection deliberately and expect to see inner and outer changes.

• Connect with other like-minded souls. This journey of being a spiritually awakened empath doesn't have to be a lonely one. It can be difficult at the beginning of your awakening to find people who deeply resonate with you. This is where finding a tribe and a mentor to help support you on the journey becomes invaluable. You'll need people who understand

and appreciate the journey you're on. Usually, these people will be easy to connect with as you start to take yoga classes or spiritually enlightening courses so don't be shy, go out there and find those who get you. In today's digitally connected world, it has never been easier for you to find those rare gems that are just like you.

Next Steps

While empaths are warm, intuitive, and compassionate people, their high level of sensitivity makes them prone to experiencing issues such as anxiety, depression, and crippling physical illnesses. The journey isn't necessarily easy if you were born to be an empath, but the good news is, you have what it takes to be an illuminating light in this world.

The first step is gaining awareness about yourself and learning what your blind spots are so you can start avoiding the traps that have been sabotaging your life so far. You've got to be courageous enough to step out of your comfort zone. Leave behind the old patterns, traumas, and lies that you've had to grow up with and step into a more liberated version of yourself. I believe this book has taken some huge strides in showing you exactly how you can step out of the victim mindset that many of us get stuck in and into a state of empowerment.

What you possess is a gift and although you may not understand it fully at this point, trust in the process of life. Learn how to develop yourself so you can stop feeling drained of your precious energy. It's time to deal with the challenges of being a highly sensitive empath in a way that empowers you and transforms the lives of those around you. It might be that life has been one continuous struggle, but from this point on, you hold the power to bring into reality a life of significant meaning filled with joy, love, great health, and success. The world needs that special gift that only you have.

Resources

Highly sensitive people Tips For Survival:
https://www.psychologytoday.com/intl/blog/prescriptions-life/201105/top-10-survival-tips-the-highly-sensitive-person-hsp

Healing emotional trauma:
http://www.chopratreatmentcenter.com/blog/2018/04/26/5-simple-steps-healing-emotional-trauma/

Meditation for beginners:
https://chopra.com/articles/start-here-5-meditation-styles-for-beginners

Finding your Dosha:
https://yogainternational.com/article/view/dosha-quiz

www.ingramcontent.com/pod-product-compliance
Lightning Source LLC
Chambersburg PA
CBHW071239070526
44583CB00017B/2252